The Winter's Tale

Cover image © 2013 by Cortney Skinner

Wilder Publications, Inc.
PO Box 632
Floyd VA 24091

ISBN 13: 978-1-5154-2480-2

First Wilder Edition
10 9 8 7 6 5 4 3 2 1

The Winter's Tale
by William Shakespeare

Dramatis Personae

LEONTES, King of Sicilia
MAMILLIUS, his son, the young Prince of Sicilia
CAMILLO, lord of Sicilia
ANTIGONUS, lord of Sicilia
CLEOMENES, lord of Sicilia
DION, lord of Sicilia
POLIXENES, King of Bohemia
FLORIZEL, his son, Prince of Bohemia
ARCHIDAMUS, a lord of Bohemia
OLD SHEPHERD, reputed father of Perdita
CLOWN, his son
AUTOLYCUS, a rogue
A MARINER
A GAOLER
TIME, as Chorus
HERMIONE, Queen to Leontes
PERDITA, daughter to Leontes and Hermione
PAULINA, wife to Antigonus
EMILIA, a lady attending on the Queen
MOPSA, shepherdess
DORCAS, shepherdess
Other Lords, Gentlemen, Ladies, Officers, Servants, Shepherds,
Shepherdesses

SCENE: *Sicilia and Bohemia*

ACT I. SCENE I. Sicilia. The Palace of Leontes
Enter Camillo and Archidamus

ARCHIDAMUS: If you shall chance, Camillo, to visit Bohemia, on the like occasion whereon my services are now on foot, you shall see, as I have said, great difference betwixt our Bohemia and your Sicilia.

CAMILLO: I think this coming summer the King of Sicilia means to pay Bohemia the visitation which he justly owes him.

ARCHIDAMUS: Wherein our entertainment shall shame us we will be justified in our loves; for indeed-

CAMILLO: Beseech you-

ARCHIDAMUS: Verily, I speak it in the freedom of my knowledge: we cannot with such magnificence, in so rare- I know not what to

SAY: We will give you sleepy drinks, that your senses, unintelligent of our insufficience, may, though they cannot praise us, as little accuse us.

CAMILLO: You pay a great deal too dear for what's given freely.

ARCHIDAMUS: Believe me, I speak as my understanding instructs me and as mine honesty puts it to utterance.

CAMILLO: Sicilia cannot show himself overkind to Bohemia. They were train'd together in their childhoods; and there rooted betwixt them then such an affection which cannot choose but branch now. Since their more mature dignities and royal necessities made separation of their society, their encounters, though not personal, have been royally attorneyed with interchange of gifts, letters, loving embassies; that they have seem'd to be together, though absent; shook hands, as over a vast; and embrac'd as it were from the ends of opposed winds. The heavens continue their loves!

ARCHIDAMUS: I think there is not in the world either malice or matter to alter it. You have an unspeakable comfort of your young Prince Mamillius; it is a gentleman of the greatest promise that ever came into my note.

CAMILLO: I very well agree with you in the hopes of him. It is a gallant child; one that indeed physics the subject, makes old hearts fresh; they that went on crutches ere he was born desire yet their life to see him a man.

ARCHIDAMUS: Would they else be content to die?

CAMILLO: Yes; if there were no other excuse why they should desire to live.

ARCHIDAMUS: If the King had no son, they would desire to live on crutches till he had one.

Exeunt

ACT I. SCENE II. Sicilia. The Palace of Leontes

Enter Leontes, Polixenes, Hermione, Mamillius, Camillo, and Attendants

POLIXENES: Nine changes of the wat'ry star hath been
The shepherd's note since we have left our throne
Without a burden. Time as long again
Would be fill'd up, my brother, with our thanks;
And yet we should for perpetuity
Go hence in debt. And therefore, like a cipher,
Yet standing in rich place, I multiply
With one 'We thank you' many thousands moe
That go before it.

LEONTES: Stay your thanks a while,
And pay them when you part.

POLIXENES: Sir, that's to-morrow.
I am question'd by my fears of what may chance
Or breed upon our absence, that may blow
No sneaping winds at home, to make us say
'This is put forth too truly.' Besides, I have stay'd
To tire your royalty.

LEONTES: We are tougher, brother,
Than you can put us to't.

POLIXENES: No longer stay.

LEONTES: One sev'night longer.

POLIXENES: Very sooth, to-morrow.

LEONTES: We'll part the time between's then; and in that

I'll no gainsaying.

POLIXENES: Press me not, beseech you, so.
There is no tongue that moves, none, none i' th' world,
So soon as yours could win me. So it should now,
Were there necessity in your request, although
'Twere needful I denied it. My affairs
Do even drag me homeward; which to hinder
Were in your love a whip to me; my stay
To you a charge and trouble. To save both,
Farewell, our brother.

LEONTES: Tongue-tied, our Queen? Speak you.

HERMIONE: I had thought, sir, to have held my peace until
You had drawn oaths from him not to stay. You, sir,
Charge him too coldly. Tell him you are sure
All in Bohemia's well- this satisfaction
The by-gone day proclaim'd. Say this to him,
He's beat from his best ward.

LEONTES: Well said, Hermione.

HERMIONE: To tell he longs to see his son were strong;
But let him say so then, and let him go;
But let him swear so, and he shall not stay;
We'll thwack him hence with distaffs.
To Polixenes Yet of your royal presence I'll
adventure the borrow of a week. When at Bohemia
You take my lord, I'll give him my commission
To let him there a month behind the gest
Prefix'd for's parting.- Yet, good deed, Leontes,
I love thee not a jar o' th' clock behind
What lady she her lord.- You'll stay?

POLIXENES: No, madam.

HERMIONE: Nay, but you will?

POLIXENES: I may not, verily.

HERMIONE: Verily!
You put me off with limber vows; but I,
Though you would seek t' unsphere the stars with oaths,
Should yet say 'Sir, no going.' Verily,
You shall not go; a lady's 'verily' is
As potent as a lord's. Will go yet?
Force me to keep you as a prisoner,
Not like a guest; so you shall pay your fees
When you depart, and save your thanks. How say you?
My prisoner or my guest? By your dread 'verily,'
One of them you shall be.

POLIXENES: Your guest, then, madam:
To be your prisoner should import offending;
Which is for me less easy to commit
Than you to punish.

HERMIONE: Not your gaoler then,
But your kind. hostess. Come, I'll question you
Of my lord's tricks and yours when you were boys.
You were pretty lordings then!

POLIXENES: We were, fair Queen,
Two lads that thought there was no more behind
But such a day to-morrow as to-day,
And to be boy eternal.

HERMIONE: Was not my lord
The verier wag o' th' two?

POLIXENES: We were as twinn'd lambs that did frisk i' th' sun
And bleat the one at th' other. What we chang'd
Was innocence for innocence; we knew not

The doctrine of ill-doing, nor dream'd
That any did. Had we pursu'd that life,
And our weak spirits ne'er been higher rear'd
With stronger blood, we should have answer'd heaven
Boldly 'Not guilty,' the imposition clear'd
Hereditary ours.

HERMIONE: By this we gather
You have tripp'd since.

POLIXENES: O my most sacred lady,
Temptations have since then been born to 's, for
In those unfledg'd days was my wife a girl;
Your precious self had then not cross'd the eyes
Of my young playfellow.

HERMIONE: Grace to boot!
Of this make no conclusion, lest you say
Your queen and I are devils. Yet, go on;
Th' offences we have made you do we'll answer,
If you first sinn'd with us, and that with us
You did continue fault, and that you slipp'd not
With any but with us.

LEONTES: Is he won yet?

HERMIONE: He'll stay, my lord.

LEONTES: At my request he would not.
Hermione, my dearest, thou never spok'st
To better purpose.

HERMIONE: Never?

LEONTES: Never but once.

HERMIONE: What! Have I twice said well? When was't before?

I prithee tell me; cram's with praise, and make's
As fat as tame things. One good deed dying tongueless
Slaughters a thousand waiting upon that.
Our praises are our wages; you may ride's
With one soft kiss a thousand furlongs ere
With spur we heat an acre. But to th' goal:
My last good deed was to entreat his stay;
What was my first? It has an elder sister,
Or I mistake you. O, would her name were Grace!
But once before I spoke to th' purpose- When?
Nay, let me have't; I long.

LEONTES: Why, that was when
Three crabbed months had sour'd themselves to death,
Ere I could make thee open thy white hand
And clap thyself my love; then didst thou utter
'I am yours for ever.'

HERMIONE: 'Tis Grace indeed.
Why, lo you now, I have spoke to th' purpose twice:
The one for ever earn'd a royal husband;
Th' other for some while a friend.
    Giving Her Hand to Polixenes

LEONTES: *Aside* Too hot, too hot!
To mingle friendship far is mingling bloods.
I have tremor cordis on me; my heart dances,
But not for joy, not joy. This entertainment
May a free face put on; derive a liberty
From heartiness, from bounty, fertile bosom,
And well become the agent. 'T may, I grant;
But to be paddling palms and pinching fingers,
As now they are, and making practis'd smiles
As in a looking-glass; and then to sigh, as 'twere
The mort o' th' deer. O, that is entertainment
My bosom likes not, nor my brows! Mamillius,
Art thou my boy?

MAMILLIUS: Ay, my good lord.

LEONTES: I' fecks!
Why, that's my bawcock. What! hast smutch'd thy nose?
They say it is a copy out of mine. Come, Captain,
We must be neat- not neat, but cleanly, Captain.
And yet the steer, the heifer, and the calf,
Are all call'd neat.- Still virginalling
Upon his palm?- How now, you wanton calf,
Art thou my calf?

MAMILLIUS: Yes, if you will, my lord.

LEONTES: Thou want'st a rough pash and the shoots that I have,
To be full like me; yet they say we are
Almost as like as eggs. Women say so,
That will say anything. But were they false
As o'er-dy'd blacks, as wind, as waters- false
As dice are to be wish'd by one that fixes
No bourn 'twixt his and mine; yet were it true
To say this boy were like me. Come, sir page,
Look on me with your welkin eye. Sweet villain!
Most dear'st! my collop! Can thy dam?- may't be?
Affection! thy intention stabs the centre.
Thou dost make possible things not so held,
Communicat'st with dreams- how can this be?-
With what's unreal thou coactive art,
And fellow'st nothing. Then 'tis very credent
Thou mayst co-join with something; and thou dost-
And that beyond commission; and I find it,
And that to the infection of my brains
And hard'ning of my brows.

POLIXENES: What means Sicilia?

HERMIONE: He something seems unsettled.

POLIXENES: How, my lord!
What cheer? How is't with you, best brother?

HERMIONE: You look
As if you held a brow of much distraction.
Are you mov'd, my lord?

LEONTES: No, in good earnest.
How sometimes nature will betray its folly,
Its tenderness, and make itself a pastime
To harder bosoms! Looking on the lines
Of my boy's face, methoughts I did recoil
Twenty-three years; and saw myself unbreech'd,
In my green velvet coat; my dagger muzzl'd,
Lest it should bite its master and so prove,
As ornaments oft do, too dangerous.
How like, methought, I then was to this kernel,
This squash, this gentleman. Mine honest friend,
Will you take eggs for money?

MAMILLIUS: No, my lord, I'll fight.

LEONTES: You will? Why, happy man be's dole! My brother,
Are you so fond of your young prince as we
Do seem to be of ours?

POLIXENES: If at home, sir,
He's all my exercise, my mirth, my matter;
Now my sworn friend, and then mine enemy;
My parasite, my soldier, statesman, all.
He makes a July's day short as December,
And with his varying childness cures in me
Thoughts that would thick my blood.

LEONTES: So stands this squire
Offic'd with me. We two will walk, my lord,
And leave you to your graver steps. Hermione,

How thou lov'st us show in our brother's welcome;
Let what is dear in Sicily be cheap;
Next to thyself and my young rover, he's
Apparent to my heart.

HERMIONE: If you would seek us,
We are yours i' th' garden. Shall's attend you there?

LEONTES: To your own bents dispose you; you'll be found,
Be you beneath the sky. *Aside* I am angling now,
Though you perceive me not how I give line.
Go to, go to!
How she holds up the neb, the bill to him!
And arms her with the boldness of a wife
To her allowing husband!
   Exeunt Polixenes, Hermione, and Attendants
Gone already!
Inch-thick, knee-deep, o'er head and ears a fork'd one!
Go, play, boy, play; thy mother plays, and I
Play too; but so disgrac'd a part, whose issue
Will hiss me to my grave. Contempt and clamour
Will be my knell. Go, play, boy, play. There have been,
Or I am much deceiv'd, cuckolds ere now;
And many a man there is, even at this present,
Now while I speak this, holds his wife by th' arm
That little thinks she has been sluic'd in's absence,
And his pond fish'd by his next neighbour, by
Sir Smile, his neighbour. Nay, there's comfort in't,
Whiles other men have gates and those gates open'd,
As mine, against their will. Should all despair
That hath revolted wives, the tenth of mankind
Would hang themselves. Physic for't there's none;
It is a bawdy planet, that will strike
Where 'tis predominant; and 'tis pow'rfull, think it,
From east, west, north, and south. Be it concluded,
No barricado for a belly. Know't,
It will let in and out the enemy

With bag and baggage. Many thousand on's
Have the disease, and feel't not. How now, boy!

MAMILLIUS: I am like you, they say.

LEONTES: Why, that's some comfort.
What! Camillo there?
CAMILLO: Ay, my good lord.

LEONTES: Go play, Mamillius; thou'rt an honest man.
  Exit Mamillius
Camillo, this great sir will yet stay longer.

CAMILLO: You had much ado to make his anchor hold;
When you cast out, it still came home.

LEONTES: Didst note it?

CAMILLO: He would not stay at your petitions; made
His business more material.

LEONTES: Didst perceive it?
Aside They're here with me already; whisp'ring, rounding,
'Sicilia is a so-forth.' 'Tis far gone
When I shall gust it last.- How came't, Camillo,
That he did stay?

CAMILLO: At the good Queen's entreaty.

LEONTES: 'At the Queen's' be't. 'Good' should be pertinent;
But so it is, it is not. Was this taken
By any understanding pate but thine?
For thy conceit is soaking, will draw in
More than the common blocks. Not noted, is't,
But of the finer natures, by some severals
Of head-piece extraordinary? Lower messes
Perchance are to this business purblind? Say.

CAMILLO: Business, my lord? I think most understand
Bohemia stays here longer.

LEONTES: Ha?

CAMILLO: Stays here longer.

LEONTES: Ay, but why?

CAMILLO: To satisfy your Highness, and the entreaties
Of our most gracious mistress.

LEONTES: Satisfy
Th' entreaties of your mistress! Satisfy!
Let that suffice. I have trusted thee, Camillo,
With all the nearest things to my heart, as well
My chamber-councils, wherein, priest-like, thou
Hast cleans'd my bosom- I from thee departed
Thy penitent reform'd; but we have been
Deceiv'd in thy integrity, deceiv'd
In that which seems so.

CAMILLO: Be it forbid, my lord!

LEONTES: To bide upon't: thou art not honest; or,
If thou inclin'st that way, thou art a coward,
Which hoxes honesty behind, restraining
From course requir'd; or else thou must be counted
A servant grafted in my serious trust,
And therein negligent; or else a fool
That seest a game play'd home, the rich stake drawn,
And tak'st it all for jest.

CAMILLO: My gracious lord,
I may be negligent, foolish, and fearful:
In every one of these no man is free
But that his negligence, his folly, fear,

Among the infinite doings of the world,
Sometime puts forth. In your affairs, my lord,
If ever I were wilfull-negligent,
It was my folly; if industriously
I play'd the fool, it was my negligence,
Not weighing well the end; if ever fearful
To do a thing where I the issue doubted,
Whereof the execution did cry out
Against the non-performance, 'twas a fear
Which oft infects the wisest. These, my lord,
Are such allow'd infirmities that honesty
Is never free of. But, beseech your Grace,
Be plainer with me; let me know my trespass
By its own visage; if I then deny it,
'Tis none of mine.

LEONTES: Ha' not you seen, Camillo-
But that's past doubt; you have, or your eye-glass
Is thicker than a cuckold's horn- or heard-
For to a vision so apparent rumour
Cannot be mute- or thought- for cogitation
Resides not in that man that does not think-
My wife is slippery? If thou wilt confess-
Or else be impudently negative,
To have nor eyes nor ears nor thought- then say
My wife's a hobby-horse, deserves a name
As rank as any flax-wench that puts to
Before her troth-plight. Say't and justify't.

CAMILLO: I would not be a stander-by to hear
My sovereign mistress clouded so, without
My present vengeance taken. Shrew my heart!
You never spoke what did become you less
Than this; which to reiterate were sin
As deep as that, though true.

LEONTES: Is whispering nothing?

Is leaning cheek to cheek? Is meeting noses?
Kissing with inside lip? Stopping the career
Of laughter with a sigh?- a note infallible
Of breaking honesty. Horsing foot on foot?
Skulking in corners? Wishing clocks more swift;
Hours, minutes; noon, midnight? And all eyes
Blind with the pin and web but theirs, theirs only,
That would unseen be wicked- is this nothing?
Why, then the world and all that's in't is nothing;
The covering sky is nothing; Bohemia nothing;
My is nothing; nor nothing have these nothings,
If this be nothing.

CAMILLO: Good my lord, be cur'd
Of this diseas'd opinion, and betimes;
For 'tis most dangerous.

LEONTES: Say it be, 'tis true.

CAMILLO: No, no, my lord.

LEONTES: It is; you lie, you lie.
I say thou liest, Camillo, and I hate thee;
Pronounce thee a gross lout, a mindless slave,
Or else a hovering temporizer that
Canst with thine eyes at once see good and evil,
Inclining to them both. Were my wife's liver
Infected as her life, she would not live
The running of one glass.

CAMILLO: Who does her?

LEONTES: Why, he that wears her like her medal, hanging
About his neck, Bohemia; who- if I
Had servants true about me that bare eyes
To see alike mine honour as their profits,
Their own particular thrifts, they would do that

Which should undo more doing. Ay, and thou,
His cupbearer- whom I from meaner form
Have bench'd and rear'd to worship; who mayst see,
Plainly as heaven sees earth and earth sees heaven,
How I am gall'd- mightst bespice a cup
To give mine enemy a lasting wink;
Which draught to me were cordial.

CAMILLO: Sir, my lord,
I could do this; and that with no rash potion,
But with a ling'ring dram that should not work
Maliciously like poison. But I cannot
Believe this crack to be in my dread mistress,
So sovereignly being honourable.
I have lov'd thee-

LEONTES: Make that thy question, and go rot!
Dost think I am so muddy, so unsettled,
To appoint myself in this vexation; sully
The purity and whiteness of my sheets-
Which to preserve is sleep, which being spotted
Is goads, thorns, nettles, tails of wasps;
Give scandal to the blood o' th' Prince, my son-
Who I do think is mine, and love as mine-
Without ripe moving to 't? Would I do this?
Could man so blench?

CAMILLO: I must believe you, sir.
I do; and will fetch off Bohemia for't;
Provided that, when he's remov'd, your Highness
Will take again your queen as yours at first,
Even for your son's sake; and thereby for sealing
The injury of tongues in courts and kingdoms
Known and allied to yours.

LEONTES: Thou dost advise me
Even so as I mine own course have set down.

I'll give no blemish to her honour, none.

CAMILLO: My lord,
Go then; and with a countenance as clear
As friendship wears at feasts, keep with Bohemia
And with your queen. I am his cupbearer;
If from me he have wholesome beverage,
Account me not your servant.

LEONTES: This is all:
Do't, and thou hast the one half of my heart;
Do't not, thou split'st thine own.

CAMILLO: I'll do't, my lord.

LEONTES: I will seem friendly, as thou hast advis'd me. *Exit*

CAMILLO: O miserable lady! But, for me,
What case stand I in? I must be the poisoner
Of good Polixenes; and my ground to do't
Is the obedience to a master; one
Who, in rebellion with himself, will have
All that are his so too. To do this deed,
Promotion follows. If I could find example
Of thousands that had struck anointed kings
And flourish'd after, I'd not do't; but since
Nor brass, nor stone, nor parchment, bears not one,
Let villainy itself forswear't. I must
Forsake the court. To do't, or no, is certain
To me a break-neck. Happy star reign now!
Here comes Bohemia.

Enter Polixenes

POLIXENES: This is strange. Methinks
My favour here begins to warp. Not speak?
Good day, Camillo.

CAMILLO: Hail, most royal sir!

POLIXENES: What is the news i' th' court?

CAMILLO: None rare, my lord.

POLIXENES: The King hath on him such a countenance
As he had lost some province, and a region
Lov'd as he loves himself; even now I met him
With customary compliment, when he,
Wafting his eyes to th' contrary and falling
A lip of much contempt, speeds from me;
So leaves me to consider what is breeding
That changes thus his manners.

CAMILLO: I dare not know, my lord.

POLIXENES: How, dare not! Do not. Do you know, and dare not
Be intelligent to me? 'Tis thereabouts;
For, to yourself, what you do know, you must,
And cannot say you dare not. Good Camillo,
Your chang'd complexions are to me a mirror
Which shows me mine chang'd too; for I must be
A party in this alteration, finding
Myself thus alter'd with't.

CAMILLO: There is a sickness
Which puts some of us in distemper; but
I cannot name the disease; and it is caught
Of you that yet are well.

POLIXENES: How! caught of me?
Make me not sighted like the basilisk;
I have look'd on thousands who have sped the better
By my regard, but kill'd none so. Camillo-
As you are certainly a gentleman; thereto
Clerk-like experienc'd, which no less adorns

Our gentry than our parents' noble names,
In whose success we are gentle- I beseech you,
If you know aught which does behove my knowledge
Thereof to be inform'd, imprison't not
In ignorant concealment.

CAMILLO: I may not answer.

POLIXENES: A sickness caught of me, and yet I well?
I must be answer'd. Dost thou hear, Camillo?
I conjure thee, by all the parts of man
Which honour does acknowledge, whereof the least
Is not this suit of mine, that thou declare
What incidency thou dost guess of harm
Is creeping toward me; how far off, how near;
Which way to be prevented, if to be;
If not, how best to bear it.

CAMILLO: Sir, I will tell you;
Since I am charg'd in honour, and by him
That I think honourable. Therefore mark my counsel,
Which must be ev'n as swiftly followed as
I mean to utter it, or both yourself and me
Cry lost, and so goodnight.

POLIXENES: On, good Camillo.

CAMILLO: I am appointed him to murder you.

POLIXENES: By whom, Camillo?

CAMILLO: By the King.

POLIXENES: For what?

CAMILLO: He thinks, nay, with all confidence he swears,
As he had seen 't or been an instrument

To vice you to't, that you have touch'd his queen
Forbiddenly.

POLIXENES: O, then my best blood turn
To an infected jelly, and my name
Be yok'd with his that did betray the Best!
Turn then my freshest reputation to
A savour that may strike the dullest nostril
Where I arrive, and my approach be shunn'd,
Nay, hated too, worse than the great'st infection
That e'er was heard or read!

CAMILLO: Swear his thought over
By each particular star in heaven and
By all their influences, you may as well
Forbid the sea for to obey the moon
As or by oath remove or counsel shake
The fabric of his folly, whose foundation
Is pil'd upon his faith and will continue
The standing of his body.

POLIXENES: How should this grow?

CAMILLO: I know not; but I am sure 'tis safer to
Avoid what's grown than question how 'tis born.
If therefore you dare trust my honesty,
That lies enclosed in this trunk which you
Shall bear along impawn'd, away to-night.
Your followers I will whisper to the business;
And will, by twos and threes, at several posterns,
Clear them o' th' city. For myself, I'll put
My fortunes to your service, which are here
By this discovery lost. Be not uncertain,
For, by the honour of my parents, I
Have utt'red truth; which if you seek to prove,
I dare not stand by; nor shall you be safer
Than one condemn'd by the King's own mouth, thereon

His execution sworn.

POLIXENES: I do believe thee:
I saw his heart in's face. Give me thy hand;
Be pilot to me, and thy places shall
Still neighbour mine. My ships are ready, and
My people did expect my hence departure
Two days ago. This jealousy
Is for a precious creature; as she's rare,
Must it be great; and, as his person's mighty,
Must it be violent; and as he does conceive
He is dishonour'd by a man which ever
Profess'd to him, why, his revenges must
In that be made more bitter. Fear o'ershades me.
Good expedition be my friend, and comfort
The gracious Queen, part of this theme, but nothing
Of his ill-ta'en suspicion! Come, Camillo;
I will respect thee as a father, if
Thou bear'st my life off hence. Let us avoid.

CAMILLO: It is in mine authority to command
The keys of all the posterns. Please your Highness
To take the urgent hour. Come, sir, away.
Exeunt

ACT II. SCENE I. Sicilia. The Palace of Leontes
Enter Hermione, Mamillius, and Ladies

HERMIONE: Take the boy to you; he so troubles me,
'Tis past enduring.

FIRST LADY: Come, my gracious lord,
Shall I be your playfellow?

MAMILLIUS: No, I'll none of you.

FIRST LADY: Why, my sweet lord?

MAMILLIUS: You'll kiss me hard, and speak to me as if
I were a baby still. I love you better.

SECOND LADY: And why so, my lord?

MAMILLIUS: Not for because
Your brows are blacker; yet black brows, they say,
Become some women best; so that there be not
Too much hair there, but in a semicircle
Or a half-moon made with a pen.

SECOND LADY: Who taught't this?

MAMILLIUS: I learn'd it out of women's faces. Pray now,
What colour are your eyebrows?

FIRST LADY: Blue, my lord.

MAMILLIUS: Nay, that's a mock. I have seen a lady's nose
That has been blue, but not her eyebrows.

FIRST LADY: Hark ye:
The Queen your mother rounds apace. We shall
Present our services to a fine new prince
One of these days; and then you'd wanton with us,
If we would have you.

SECOND LADY: She is spread of late
Into a goodly bulk. Good time encounter her!

HERMIONE: What wisdom stirs amongst you? Come, sir, now
I am for you again. Pray you sit by us,
And tell's a tale.

MAMILLIUS: Merry or sad shall't be?

HERMIONE: As merry as you will.

MAMILLIUS: A sad tale's best for winter. I have one
Of sprites and goblins.

HERMIONE: Let's have that, good sir.
Come on, sit down; come on, and do your best
To fright me with your sprites; you're pow'rfull at it.

MAMILLIUS: There was a man-

HERMIONE: Nay, come, sit down; then on.

MAMILLIUS: Dwelt by a churchyard- I will tell it softly;
Yond crickets shall not hear it.

HERMIONE: Come on then,
And give't me in mine ear.
   Enter Leontes, Antigonus, Lords, and Others

LEONTES: he met there? his train? Camillo with him?

FIRST LORD: Behind the tuft of pines I met them; never
Saw I men scour so on their way. I ey'd them
Even to their ships.

LEONTES: How blest am I
In my just censure, in my true opinion!
Alack, for lesser knowledge! How accurs'd
In being so blest! There may be in the cup
A spider steep'd, and one may drink, depart,
And yet partake no venom, for his knowledge
Is not infected; but if one present
Th' abhorr'd ingredient to his eye, make known
How he hath drunk, he cracks his gorge, his sides,
With violent hefts. I have drunk, and seen the spider.
Camillo was his help in this, his pander.

There is a plot against my life, my crown;
All's true that is mistrusted. That false villain
Whom I employ'd was pre-employ'd by him;
He has discover'd my design, and I
Remain a pinch'd thing; yea, a very trick
For them to play at will. How came the posterns
So easily open?

FIRST LORD: By his great authority;
Which often hath no less prevail'd than so
On your command.

LEONTES: I know't too well.
Give me the boy. I am glad you did not nurse him;
Though he does bear some signs of me, yet you
Have too much blood in him.

HERMIONE: What is this? Sport?

LEONTES: Bear the boy hence; he shall not come about her;
Away with him; and let her sport herself
   Mamillius Is Led Out
With that she's big with- for 'tis Polixenes
Has made thee swell thus.

HERMIONE: But I'd say he had not,
And I'll be sworn you would believe my saying,
Howe'er you lean to th' nayward.

LEONTES: You, my lords,
Look on her, mark her well; be but about
To say 'She is a goodly lady' and
The justice of your hearts will thereto ad
'Tis pity she's not honest- honourable.'
Praise her but for this her without-door form,
Which on my faith deserves high speech, and straight
The shrug, the hum or ha, these petty brands

That calumny doth use- O, I am out!-
That mercy does, for calumny will sear
Virtue itself- these shrugs, these hum's and ha's,
When you have said she's goodly, come between,
Ere you can say she's honest. But be't known,
From him that has most cause to grieve it should be,
She's an adultress.

HERMIONE: Should a villain say so,
The most replenish'd villain in the world,
He were as much more villain: you, my lord,
Do but mistake.

LEONTES: You have mistook, my lady,
Polixenes for Leontes. O thou thing!
Which I'll not call a creature of thy place,
Lest barbarism, making me the precedent,
Should a like language use to all degrees
And mannerly distinguishment leave out
Betwixt the prince and beggar. I have said
She's an adultress; I have said with whom.
More, she's a traitor; and Camillo is
A federary with her, and one that knows
What she should shame to know herself
But with her most vile principal- that she's
A bed-swerver, even as bad as those
That vulgars give bold'st titles; ay, and privy
To this their late escape.

HERMIONE: No, by my life,
Privy to none of this. How will this grieve you,
When you shall come to clearer knowledge, that
You thus have publish'd me! Gentle my lord,
You scarce can right me throughly then to say
You did mistake.

LEONTES: No; if I mistake

In those foundations which I build upon,
The centre is not big enough to bear
A school-boy's top. Away with her to prison.
He who shall speak for her is afar off guilty
But that he speaks.

HERMIONE: There's some ill planet reigns.
I must be patient till the heavens look
With an aspect more favourable. Good my lords,
I am not prone to weeping, as our sex
Commonly are- the want of which vain dew
Perchance shall dry your pities- but I have
That honourable grief lodg'd here which burns
Worse than tears drown. Beseech you all, my lords,
With thoughts so qualified as your charities
Shall best instruct you, measure me; and so
The King's will be perform'd!

LEONTES: *To the Guard* Shall I be heard?

HERMIONE: Who is't that goes with me? Beseech your highness
My women may be with me, for you see
My plight requires it. Do not weep, good fools;
There is no cause; when you shall know your mistress
Has deserv'd prison, then abound in tears
As I come out: this action I now go on
Is for my better grace. Adieu, my lord.
I never wish'd to see you sorry; now
I trust I shall. My women, come; you have leave.

LEONTES: Go, do our bidding; hence!
  Exeunt Hermione, Guarded, and Ladies

FIRST LORD: Beseech your Highness, call the Queen again.

ANTIGONUS: Be certain what you do, sir, lest your justice
Prove violence, in the which three great ones suffer,

Yourself, your queen, your son.

FIRST LORD: For her, my lord,
I dare my life lay down- and will do't, sir,
Please you t' accept it- that the Queen is spotless
I' th' eyes of heaven and to you- I mean
In this which you accuse her.

ANTIGONUS: If it prove
She's otherwise, I'll keep my stables where
I lodge my wife; I'll go in couples with her;
Than when I feel and see her no farther trust her;
For every inch of woman in the world,
Ay, every dram of woman's flesh is false,
If she be.

LEONTES: Hold your peaces.

FIRST LORD: Good my lord-

ANTIGONUS: It is for you we speak, not for ourselves.
You are abus'd, and by some putter-on
That will be damn'd for't. Would I knew the villain!
I would land-damn him. Be she honour-flaw'd-
I have three daughters: the eldest is eleven;
The second and the third, nine and some five;
If this prove true, they'll pay for 't. By mine honour,
I'll geld 'em all; fourteen they shall not see
To bring false generations. They are co-heirs;
And I had rather glib myself than they
Should not produce fair issue.

LEONTES: Cease; no more.
You smell this business with a sense as cold
As is a dead man's nose; but I do see't and feel't
As you feel doing thus; and see withal
The instruments that feel.

ANTIGONUS: If it be so,
We need no grave to bury honesty;
There's not a grain of it the face to sweeten
Of the whole dungy earth.

LEONTES: What! Lack I credit?

FIRST LORD: I had rather you did lack than I, my lord,
Upon this ground; and more it would content me
To have her honour true than your suspicion,
Be blam'd for't how you might.

LEONTES: Why, what need we
Commune with you of this, but rather follow
Our forceful instigation? Our prerogative
Calls not your counsels; but our natural goodness
Imparts this; which, if you- or stupified
Or seeming so in skill- cannot or will not
Relish a truth like us, inform yourselves
We need no more of your advice. The matter,
The loss, the gain, the ord'ring on't, is all
Properly ours.

ANTIGONUS: And I wish, my liege,
You had only in your silent judgment tried it,
Without more overture.

LEONTES: How could that be?
Either thou art most ignorant by age,
Or thou wert born a fool. Camillo's flight,
Added to their familiarity-
Which was as gross as ever touch'd conjecture,
That lack'd sight only, nought for approbation
But only seeing, all other circumstances
Made up to th' deed- doth push on this proceeding.
Yet, for a greater confirmation-
For, in an act of this importance, 'twere

Most piteous to be wild- I have dispatch'd in post
To sacred Delphos, to Apollo's temple,
Cleomenes and Dion, whom you know
Of stuff'd sufficiency. Now, from the oracle
They will bring all, whose spiritual counsel had,
Shall stop or spur me. Have I done well?

FIRST LORD: Well done, my lord.

LEONTES: Though I am satisfied, and need no more
Than what I know, yet shall the oracle
Give rest to th' minds of others such as he
Whose ignorant credulity will not
Come up to th' truth. So have we thought it good
From our free person she should be confin'd,
Lest that the treachery of the two fled hence
Be left her to perform. Come, follow us;
We are to speak in public; for this business
Will raise us all.

ANTIGONUS: *Aside* To laughter, as I take it,
If the good truth were known.
   Exeunt

ACT II. SCENE II. Sicilia. A Prison
Enter Paulina, a Gentleman, and Attendants

ANTIGONUS: The keeper of the prison- call to him;
Let him have knowledge who I am.
   Exit Gentleman
Good lady!
No court in Europe is too good for thee;
What dost thou then in prison?
   Re-enter Gentleman with the Gaoler
Now, good sir,
You know me, do you not?

GAOLER: For a worthy lady,
And one who much I honour.

ANTIGONUS: Pray you, then,
Conduct me to the Queen.

GAOLER: I may not, madam;
To the contrary I have express commandment.

ANTIGONUS: Here's ado, to lock up honesty and honour from
Th' access of gentle visitors! Is't lawful, pray you,
To see her women- any of them? Emilia?

GAOLER: So please you, madam,
To put apart these your attendants,
Shall bring Emilia forth.

ANTIGONUS: I pray now, call her.
Withdraw yourselves.
    Exeunt Attendants

GAOLER: And, madam,
I must be present at your conference.

ANTIGONUS: Well, be't so, prithee.
    Exit Gaoler
Here's such ado to make no stain a stain
As passes colouring.
    Re-enter Gaoler, with Emilia
Dear gentlewoman,
How fares our gracious lady?

EMILIA: As well as one so great and so forlorn
May hold together. On her frights and griefs,
Which never tender lady hath borne greater,
She is, something before her time, deliver'd.

ANTIGONUS: A boy?

EMILIA: A daughter, and a goodly babe,
Lusty, and like to live. The Queen receives
Much comfort in't; says 'My poor prisoner,
I am as innocent as you.'

ANTIGONUS: I dare be sworn.
These dangerous unsafe lunes i' th' King, beshrew them!
He must be told on't, and he shall. The office
Becomes a woman best; I'll take't upon me;
If I prove honey-mouth'd, let my tongue blister,
And never to my red-look'd anger be
The trumpet any more. Pray you, Emilia,
Commend my best obedience to the Queen;
If she dares trust me with her little babe,
I'll show't the King, and undertake to be
Her advocate to th' loud'st. We do not know
How he may soften at the sight o' th' child:
The silence often of pure innocence
Persuades when speaking fails.

EMILIA: Most worthy madam,
Your honour and your goodness is so evident
That your free undertaking cannot miss
A thriving issue; there is no lady living
So meet for this great errand. Please your ladyship
To visit the next room, I'll presently
Acquaint the Queen of your most noble offer
Who but to-day hammer'd of this design,
But durst not tempt a minister of honour,
Lest she should be denied.

ANTIGONUS: Tell her, Emilia,
I'll use that tongue I have; if wit flow from't
As boldness from my bosom, let't not be doubted
I shall do good.

EMILIA: Now be you blest for it!
I'll to the Queen. Please you come something nearer.

GAOLER: Madam, if't please the Queen to send the babe,
I know not what I shall incur to pass it,
Having no warrant.

ANTIGONUS: You need not fear it, sir.
This child was prisoner to the womb, and is
By law and process of great Nature thence
Freed and enfranchis'd- not a party to
The anger of the King, nor guilty of,
If any be, the trespass of the Queen.

GAOLER: I do believe it.

ANTIGONUS: Do not you fear. Upon mine honour, I
Will stand betwixt you and danger.
Exeunt

ACT II. SCENE III. Sicilia. The Palace of Leontes
Enter Leontes, Antigonus, Lords, and Servants

LEONTES: Nor night nor day no rest! It is but weakness
To bear the matter thus- mere weakness. If
The cause were not in being- part o' th' cause,
She, th' adultress; for the harlot king
Is quite beyond mine arm, out of the blank
And level of my brain, plot-proof; but she
I can hook to me- say that she were gone,
Given to the fire, a moiety of my rest
Might come to me again. Who's there?

FIRST SERVANT: My lord?

LEONTES: How does the boy?

FIRST SERVANT: He took good rest to-night;
'Tis hop'd his sickness is discharg'd.

LEONTES: To see his nobleness!
Conceiving the dishonour of his mother,
He straight declin'd, droop'd, took it deeply,
Fasten'd and fix'd the shame on't in himself,
Threw off his spirit, his appetite, his sleep,
And downright languish'd. Leave me solely. Go,
See how he fares.
  Exit Servant
Fie, fie! no thought of him!
The very thought of my revenges that way
Recoil upon me- in himself too mighty,
And in his parties, his alliance. Let him be,
Until a time may serve; for present vengeance,
Take it on her. Camillo and Polixenes
Laugh at me, make their pastime at my sorrow.
They should not laugh if I could reach them; nor
Shall she, within my pow'r.
  Enter Paulina, with a Child

FIRST LORD: You must not enter.

ANTIGONUS: Nay, rather, good my lords, be second to me.
Fear you his tyrannous passion more, alas,
Than the Queen's life? A gracious innocent soul,
More free than he is jealous.

ANTIGONUS: That's enough.

SECOND SERVANT: Madam, he hath not slept to-night; commanded
None should come at him.

ANTIGONUS: Not so hot, good sir;
I come to bring him sleep. 'Tis such as you,
That creep like shadows by him, and do sigh

At each his needless heavings- such as you
Nourish the cause of his awaking: I
Do come with words as medicinal as true,
Honest as either, to purge him of that humour
That presses him from sleep.

LEONTES: What noise there, ho?

ANTIGONUS: No noise, my lord; but needful conference
About some gossips for your Highness.

LEONTES: How!
Away with that audacious lady! Antigonus,
I charg'd thee that she should not come about me;
I knew she would.

ANTIGONUS: I told her so, my lord,
On your displeasure's peril, and on mine,
She should not visit you.

LEONTES: What, canst not rule her?

ANTIGONUS: From all dishonesty he can: in this,
Unless he take the course that you have done-
Commit me for committing honour- trust it,
He shall not rule me.

ANTIGONUS: La you now, you hear!
When she will take the rein, I let her run;
But she'll not stumble.

ANTIGONUS: Good my liege, I come-
And I beseech you hear me, who professes
Myself your loyal servant, your physician,
Your most obedient counsellor; yet that dares
Less appear so, in comforting your evils,
Than such as most seem yours- I say I come

From your good Queen.

LEONTES: Good Queen!

ANTIGONUS: Good Queen, my lord, good Queen- I say good Queen;
And would by combat make her good, so were I
A man, the worst about you.

LEONTES: Force her hence.

ANTIGONUS: Let him that makes but trifles of his eyes
First hand me. On mine own accord I'll off;
But first I'll do my errand. The good Queen,
For she is good, hath brought you forth a daughter;
Here 'tis; commends it to your blessing.
    Laying down the Child

LEONTES: Out!
A mankind witch! Hence with her, out o' door!
A most intelligencing bawd!

ANTIGONUS: Not so.
I am as ignorant in that as you
In so entitling me; and no less honest
Than you are mad; which is enough, I'll warrant,
As this world goes, to pass for honest.

LEONTES: Traitors!
Will you not push her out? Give her the bastard.
To Antigonus Thou dotard, thou art woman-tir'd, unroosted
By thy Dame Partlet here. Take up the bastard;
Take't up, I say; give't to thy crone.

ANTIGONUS: For ever
Unvenerable be thy hands, if thou
Tak'st up the Princess by that forced baseness
Which he has put upon't!

LEONTES: He dreads his wife.

ANTIGONUS: So I would you did; then 'twere past all doubt
You'd call your children yours.

LEONTES: A nest of traitors!

ANTIGONUS: I am none, by this good light.

ANTIGONUS: Nor I; nor any
But one that's here; and that's himself; for he
The sacred honour of himself, his Queen's,
His hopeful son's, his babe's, betrays to slander,
Whose sting is sharper than the sword's; and will not-
For, as the case now stands, it is a curse
He cannot be compell'd to 't- once remove
The root of his opinion, which is rotten
As ever oak or stone was sound.

LEONTES: A callat
Of boundless tongue, who late hath beat her husband,
And now baits me! This brat is none of mine;
It is the issue of Polixenes.
Hence with it, and together with the dam
Commit them to the fire.

ANTIGONUS: It is yours.
And, might we lay th' old proverb to your charge,
So like you 'tis the worse. Behold, my lords,
Although the print be little, the whole matter
And copy of the father- eye, nose, lip,
The trick of's frown, his forehead; nay, the valley,
The pretty dimples of his chin and cheek; his smiles;
The very mould and frame of hand, nail, finger.
And thou, good goddess Nature, which hast made it
So like to him that got it, if thou hast
The ordering of the mind too, 'mongst all colours

No yellow in't, lest she suspect, as he does,
Her children not her husband's!

LEONTES: A gross hag!
And, lozel, thou art worthy to be hang'd
That wilt not stay her tongue.

ANTIGONUS: Hang all the husbands
That cannot do that feat, you'll leave yourself
Hardly one subject.

LEONTES: Once more, take her hence.

ANTIGONUS: A most unworthy and unnatural lord
Can do no more.

LEONTES: I'll ha' thee burnt.

ANTIGONUS: I care not.
It is an heretic that makes the fire,
Not she which burns in't. I'll not call you tyrant
But this most cruel usage of your Queen-
Not able to produce more accusation
Than your own weak-hing'd fancy- something savours
Of tyranny, and will ignoble make you,
Yea, scandalous to the world.

LEONTES: On your allegiance,
Out of the chamber with her! Were I a tyrant,
Where were her life? She durst not call me so,
If she did know me one. Away with her!

ANTIGONUS: I pray you, do not push me; I'll be gone.
Look to your babe, my lord; 'tis yours. Jove send her
A better guiding spirit! What needs these hands?
You that are thus so tender o'er his follies
Will never do him good, not one of you.

So, so. Farewell; we are gone.
Exit

LEONTES: Thou, traitor, hast set on thy wife to this.
My child! Away with't. Even thou, that hast
A heart so tender o'er it, take it hence,
And see it instantly consum'd with fire;
Even thou, and none but thou. Take it up straight.
Within this hour bring me word 'tis done,
And by good testimony, or I'll seize thy life,
With that thou else call'st thine. If thou refuse,
And wilt encounter with my wrath, say so;
The bastard brains with these my proper hands
Shall I dash out. Go, take it to the fire;
For thou set'st on thy wife.

ANTIGONUS: I did not, sir.
These lords, my noble fellows, if they please,
Can clear me in't.

LORDS: We can. My royal liege,
He is not guilty of her coming hither.

LEONTES: You're liars all.

FIRST LORD: Beseech your Highness, give us better credit.
We have always truly serv'd you; and beseech
So to esteem of us; and on our knees we beg,
As recompense of our dear services
Past and to come, that you do change this purpose,
Which being so horrible, so bloody, must
Lead on to some foul issue. We all kneel.

LEONTES: I am a feather for each wind that blows.
Shall I live on to see this bastard kneel
And call me father? Better burn it now
Than curse it then. But be it; let it live.

It shall not neither.
To Antigonus You, Sir, come you hither.
You that have been so tenderly officious
With Lady Margery, your midwife there,
To save this bastard's life- for 'tis a bastard,
So sure as this beard's grey- what will you adventure
To save this brat's life?

ANTIGONUS: Anything, my lord,
That my ability may undergo,
And nobleness impose. At least, thus much:
I'll pawn the little blood which I have left
To save the innocent- anything possible.

LEONTES: It shall be possible. Swear by this sword
Thou wilt perform my bidding.

ANTIGONUS: I will, my lord.

LEONTES: Mark, and perform it- seest thou? For the fail
Of any point in't shall not only be
Death to thyself, but to thy lewd-tongu'd wife,
Whom for this time we pardon. We enjoin thee,
As thou art liegeman to us, that thou carry
This female bastard hence; and that thou bear it
To some remote and desert place, quite out
Of our dominions; and that there thou leave it,
Without more mercy, to it own protection
And favour of the climate. As by strange fortune
It came to us, I do in justice charge thee,
On thy soul's peril and thy body's torture,
That thou commend it strangely to some place
Where chance may nurse or end it. Take it up.

ANTIGONUS: I swear to do this, though a present death
Had been more merciful. Come on, poor babe.
Some powerful spirit instruct the kites and ravens

To be thy nurses! Wolves and bears, they say,
Casting their savageness aside, have done
Like offices of pity. Sir, be prosperous
In more than this deed does require! And blessing
Against this cruelty fight on thy side,
Poor thing, condemn'd to loss!
Exit with the Child

LEONTES: No, I'll not rear
Another's issue.
Enter a Servant

SERVANT: Please your Highness, posts
From those you sent to th' oracle are come
An hour since. Cleomenes and Dion,
Being well arriv'd from Delphos, are both landed,
Hasting to th' court.

FIRST LORD: So please you, sir, their speed
Hath been beyond account.

LEONTES: Twenty-three days
They have been absent; 'tis good speed; foretells
The great Apollo suddenly will have
The truth of this appear. Prepare you, lords;
Summon a session, that we may arraign
Our most disloyal lady; for, as she hath
Been publicly accus'd, so shall she have
A just and open trial. While she lives,
My heart will be a burden to me. Leave me;
And think upon my bidding.
Exeunt

ACT III. SCENE I. Sicilia. On the Road to the Capital
Enter Cleomenes and Dion

CLEOMENES: The climate's delicate, the air most sweet,

Fertile the isle, the temple much surpassing
The common praise it bears.

DION: I shall report,
For most it caught me, the celestial habits-
Methinks I so should term them- and the reverence
Of the grave wearers. O, the sacrifice!
How ceremonious, solemn, and unearthly,
It was i' th' off'ring!

CLEOMENES: But of all, the burst
And the ear-deaf'ning voice o' th' oracle,
Kin to Jove's thunder, so surpris'd my sense
That I was nothing.

DION: If th' event o' th' journey
Prove as successful to the Queen- O, be't so!-
As it hath been to us rare, pleasant, speedy,
The time is worth the use on't.

CLEOMENES: Great Apollo
Turn all to th' best! These proclamations,
So forcing faults upon Hermione,
I little like.

DION: The violent carriage of it
Will clear or end the business. When the oracle-
Thus by Apollo's great divine seal'd up-
Shall the contents discover, something rare
Even then will rush to knowledge. Go; fresh horses.
And gracious be the issue!
  Exeunt

ACT III. SCENE II. Sicilia. A court of Justice
Enter Leontes, Lords, and Officers

LEONTES: This sessions, to our great grief we pronounce,

Even pushes 'gainst our heart- the party tried,
The daughter of a king, our wife, and one
Of us too much belov'd. Let us be clear'd
Of being tyrannous, since we so openly
Proceed in justice, which shall have due course,
Even to the guilt or the purgation.
Produce the prisoner.

OFFICER: It is his Highness' pleasure that the Queen
Appear in person here in court.
  Enter Hermione, as to Her Trial, Paulina, and Ladies
Silence!

LEONTES: Read the indictment.

OFFICER: *Reads* 'Hermione, Queen to the worthy Leontes, King of Sicilia,
thou art here accused and arraigned of high treason, in committing adultery
with Polixenes, King of Bohemia; and conspiring with Camillo to take away
the life of our sovereign lord the King, thy royal husband: the pretence
whereof being by circumstances partly laid open, thou, Hermione, contrary
to the faith and allegiance of true subject, didst counsel and aid them, for
their better safety, to fly away by night.'

HERMIONE: Since what I am to say must be but that
Which contradicts my accusation, and
The testimony on my part no other
But what comes from myself, it shall scarce boot me
To say 'Not guilty.' Mine integrity
Being counted falsehood shall, as I express it,
Be so receiv'd. But thus- if pow'rs divine
Behold our human actions, as they do,
I doubt not then but innocence shall make
False accusation blush, and tyranny
Tremble at patience. You, my lord, best know-
Who least will seem to do so- my past life
Hath been as continent, as chaste, as true,
As I am now unhappy; which is more

Than history can pattern, though devis'd
And play'd to take spectators; for behold me-
A fellow of the royal bed, which owe
A moiety of the throne, a great king's daughter,
The mother to a hopeful prince- here standing
To prate and talk for life and honour fore
Who please to come and hear. For life, I prize it
As I weigh grief, which I would spare; for honour,
'Tis a derivative from me to mine,
And only that I stand for. I appeal
To your own conscience, sir, before Polixenes
Came to your court, how I was in your grace,
How merited to be so; since he came,
With what encounter so uncurrent I
Have strain'd t' appear thus; if one jot beyond
The bound of honour, or in act or will
That way inclining, hard'ned be the hearts
Of all that hear me, and my near'st of kin
Cry fie upon my grave!

LEONTES: I ne'er heard yet
That any of these bolder vices wanted
Less impudence to gainsay what they did
Than to perform it first.

HERMIONE: That's true enough;
Though 'tis a saying, sir, not due to me.

LEONTES: You will not own it.

HERMIONE: More than mistress of
Which comes to me in name of fault, I must not
At all acknowledge. For Polixenes,
With whom I am accus'd, I do confess
I lov'd him as in honour he requir'd;
With such a kind of love as might become
A lady like me; with a love even such,

So and no other, as yourself commanded;
Which not to have done, I think had been in me
Both disobedience and ingratitude
To you and toward your friend; whose love had spoke,
Ever since it could speak, from an infant, freely,
That it was yours. Now for conspiracy:
I know not how it tastes, though it be dish'd
For me to try how; all I know of it
Is that Camillo was an honest man;
And why he left your court, the gods themselves,
Wotting no more than I, are ignorant.

LEONTES: You knew of his departure, as you know
What you have underta'en to do in's absence.

HERMIONE: Sir,
You speak a language that I understand not.
My life stands in the level of your dreams,
Which I'll lay down.

LEONTES: Your actions are my dreams.
You had a bastard by Polixenes,
And I but dream'd it. As you were past all shame-
Those of your fact are so- so past all truth;
Which to deny concerns more than avails; for as
Thy brat hath been cast out, like to itself,
No father owning it- which is indeed
More criminal in thee than it- so thou
Shalt feel our justice; in whose easiest passage
Look for no less than death.

HERMIONE: Sir, spare your threats.
The bug which you would fright me with I seek.
To me can life be no commodity.
The crown and comfort of my life, your favour,
I do give lost, for I do feel it gone,
But know not how it went; my second joy

And first fruits of my body, from his presence
I am barr'd, like one infectious; my third comfort,
Starr'd most unluckily, is from my breast-
The innocent milk in it most innocent mouth-
Hal'd out to murder; myself on every post
Proclaim'd a strumpet; with immodest hatred
The child-bed privilege denied, which 'longs
To women of all fashion; lastly, hurried
Here to this place, i' th' open air, before
I have got strength of limit. Now, my liege,
Tell me what blessings I have here alive
That I should fear to die. Therefore proceed.
But yet hear this- mistake me not: no life,
I prize it not a straw, but for mine honour
Which I would free- if I shall be condemn'd
Upon surmises, all proofs sleeping else
But what your jealousies awake, I tell you
'Tis rigour, and not law. Your honours all,
I do refer me to the oracle:
Apollo be my judge!

FIRST LORD: This your request
Is altogether just. Therefore, bring forth,
And in Apollo's name, his oracle.
  Exeunt Certain Officers

HERMIONE: The Emperor of Russia was my father;
O that he were alive, and here beholding
His daughter's trial! that he did but see
The flatness of my misery; yet with eyes
Of pity, not revenge!
  Re-enter Officers, with Cleomenes and Dion

OFFICER: You here shall swear upon this sword of justice
That you, Cleomenes and Dion, have
Been both at Delphos, and from thence have brought
This seal'd-up oracle, by the hand deliver'd

Of great Apollo's priest; and that since then
You have not dar'd to break the holy seal
Nor read the secrets in't.

CLEOMENES, DION: All this we swear.

LEONTES: Break up the seals and read.

OFFICER: *Reads* 'Hermione is chaste; Polixenes blameless;
Camillo a true subject; Leontes a jealous tyrant; his innocent
babe truly begotten; and the King shall live without an heir, if
that which is lost be not found.'

LORDS: Now blessed be the great Apollo!

HERMIONE: Praised!

LEONTES: Hast thou read truth?

OFFICER: Ay, my lord; even so
As it is here set down.

LEONTES: There is no truth at all i' th' oracle.
The sessions shall proceed. This is mere falsehood.
    Enter a Servant

SERVANT: My lord the King, the King!

LEONTES: What is the business?

SERVANT: O sir, I shall be hated to report it:
The Prince your son, with mere conceit and fear
Of the Queen's speed, is gone.

LEONTES: How! Gone?

SERVANT: Is dead.

LEONTES: Apollo's angry; and the heavens themselves
Do strike at my injustice. *Hermione Swoons*
How now, there!

ANTIGONUS: This news is mortal to the Queen. Look down
And see what death is doing.

LEONTES: Take her hence.
Her heart is but o'ercharg'd; she will recover.
I have too much believ'd mine own suspicion.
Beseech you tenderly apply to her
Some remedies for life.
　　Exeunt Paulina and Ladies with Hermione
Apollo, pardon
My great profaneness 'gainst thine oracle.
I'll reconcile me to Polixenes,
New woo my queen, recall the good Camillo-
Whom I proclaim a man of truth, of mercy.
For, being transported by my jealousies
To bloody thoughts and to revenge, I chose
Camillo for the minister to poison
My friend Polixenes; which had been done
But that the good mind of Camillo tardied
My swift command, though I with death and with
Reward did threaten and encourage him,
Not doing it and being done. He, most humane
And fill'd with honour, to my kingly guest
Unclasp'd my practice, quit his fortunes here,
Which you knew great, and to the certain hazard
Of all incertainties himself commended,
No richer than his honour. How he glisters
Thorough my rust! And how his piety
Does my deeds make the blacker!
　　Re-enter Paulina

ANTIGONUS: Woe the while!
O, cut my lace, lest my heart, cracking it,

Break too!

FIRST LORD: What fit is this, good lady?

ANTIGONUS: What studied torments, tyrant, hast for me?
What wheels, racks, fires? what flaying, boiling
In leads or oils? What old or newer torture
Must I receive, whose every word deserves
To taste of thy most worst? Thy tyranny
Together working with thy jealousies,
Fancies too weak for boys, too green and idle
For girls of nine- O, think what they have done,
And then run mad indeed, stark mad; for all
Thy by-gone fooleries were but spices of it.
That thou betray'dst Polixenes, 'twas nothing;
That did but show thee, of a fool, inconstant,
And damnable ingrateful. Nor was't much
Thou wouldst have poison'd good Camillo's honour,
To have him kill a king- poor trespasses,
More monstrous standing by; whereof I reckon
The casting forth to crows thy baby daughter
To be or none or little, though a devil
Would have shed water out of fire ere done't;
Nor is't directly laid to thee, the death
Of the young Prince, whose honourable thoughts-
Thoughts high for one so tender- cleft the heart
That could conceive a gross and foolish sire
Blemish'd his gracious dam. This is not, no,
Laid to thy answer; but the last- O lords,
When I have said, cry 'Woe!'- the Queen, the Queen,
The sweet'st, dear'st creature's dead; and vengeance
For't not dropp'd down yet.

FIRST LORD: The higher pow'rs forbid!

ANTIGONUS: I say she's dead; I'll swear't. If word nor oath
Prevail not, go and see. If you can bring

Tincture or lustre in her lip, her eye,
Heat outwardly or breath within, I'll serve you
As I would do the gods. But, O thou tyrant!
Do not repent these things, for they are heavier
Than all thy woes can stir; therefore betake thee
To nothing but despair. A thousand knees
Ten thousand years together, naked, fasting,
Upon a barren mountain, and still winter
In storm perpetual, could not move the gods
To look that way thou wert.

LEONTES: Go on, go on.
Thou canst not speak too much; I have deserv'd
All tongues to talk their bitt'rest.

FIRST LORD: Say no more;
Howe'er the business goes, you have made fault
I' th' boldness of your speech.

ANTIGONUS: I am sorry for't.
All faults I make, when I shall come to know them.
I do repent. Alas, I have show'd too much
The rashness of a woman! He is touch'd
To th' noble heart. What's gone and what's past help
Should be past grief. Do not receive affliction
At my petition; I beseech you, rather
Let me be punish'd that have minded you
Of what you should forget. Now, good my liege,
Sir, royal sir, forgive a foolish woman.
The love I bore your queen- lo, fool again!
I'll speak of her no more, nor of your children;
I'll not remember you of my own lord,
Who is lost too. Take your patience to you,
And I'll say nothing.

LEONTES: Thou didst speak but well
When most the truth; which I receive much better

Than to be pitied of thee. Prithee, bring me
To the dead bodies of my queen and son.
One grave shall be for both. Upon them shall
The causes of their death appear, unto
Our shame perpetual. Once a day I'll visit
The chapel where they lie; and tears shed there
Shall be my recreation. So long as nature
Will bear up with this exercise, so long
I daily vow to use it. Come, and lead me
To these sorrows.
  Exeunt

ACT III. SCENE III. Bohemia. The Sea-Coast
Enter Antigonus with the Child, and a Mariner

ANTIGONUS: Thou art perfect then our ship hath touch'd upon
The deserts of Bohemia?

MARINER: Ay, my lord, and fear
We have landed in ill time; the skies look grimly
And threaten present blusters. In my conscience,
The heavens with that we have in hand are angry
And frown upon 's.

ANTIGONUS: Their sacred wills be done! Go, get aboard;
Look to thy bark. I'll not be long before
I call upon thee.

MARINER: Make your best haste; and go not
Too far i' th' land; 'tis like to be loud weather;
Besides, this place is famous for the creatures
Of prey that keep upon't.

ANTIGONUS: Go thou away;
I'll follow instantly.

MARINER: I am glad at heart

To be so rid o' th' business.
　Exit

ANTIGONUS: Come, poor babe.
I have heard, but not believ'd, the spirits o' th' dead
May walk again. If such thing be, thy mother
Appear'd to me last night; for ne'er was dream
So like a waking. To me comes a creature,
Sometimes her head on one side some another-
I never saw a vessel of like sorrow,
So fill'd and so becoming; in pure white robes,
Like very sanctity, she did approach
My cabin where I lay; thrice bow'd before me;
And, gasping to begin some speech, her eyes
Became two spouts; the fury spent, anon
Did this break from her: 'Good Antigonus,
Since fate, against thy better disposition,
Hath made thy person for the thrower-out
Of my poor babe, according to thine oath,
Places remote enough are in Bohemia,
There weep, and leave it crying; and, for the babe
Is counted lost for ever, Perdita
I prithee call't. For this ungentle business,
Put on thee by my lord, thou ne'er shalt see
Thy wife Paulina more.' so, with shrieks,
She melted into air. Affrighted much,
I did in time collect myself, and thought
This was so and no slumber. Dreams are toys;
Yet, for this once, yea, superstitiously,
I will be squar'd by this. I do believe
Hermione hath suffer'd death, and that
Apollo would, this being indeed the issue
Of King Polixenes, it should here be laid,
Either for life or death, upon the earth
Of its right father. Blossom, speed thee well!
　Laying down the Child
There lie, and there thy character; there these

Laying down a Bundle
Which may, if fortune please, both breed thee, pretty,
And still rest thine. The storm begins. Poor wretch,
That for thy mother's fault art thus expos'd
To loss and what may follow! Weep I cannot,
But my heart bleeds; and most accurs'd am I
To be by oath enjoin'd to this. Farewell!
The day frowns more and more. Thou'rt like to have
A lullaby too rough; I never saw
The heavens so dim by day. *Noise of Hunt Within*
A savage clamour!
Well may I get aboard! This is the chase;
I am gone for ever. *Exit, Pursued by a Bear*
Enter an Old Shepherd

SHEPHERD: I would there were no age between ten and three and twenty, or that youth would sleep out the rest; for there is nothing in the between but getting wenches with child, wronging the ancientry, stealing, fighting- *Horns* Hark you now! Would any but these boil'd brains of nineteen and two and twenty hunt this weather? They have scar'd away two of my best sheep, which I fear the wolf will sooner find than the master. If any where I have them, 'tis by the sea-side, browsing of ivy. Good luck, an't be thy will! What have we here? *Taking up the Child* Mercy on's, a barne! A very pretty barne. A boy or a child, I wonder? A pretty one; a very pretty one- sure, some scape. Though I am not bookish, yet I can read waiting-gentlewoman in the scape. This has been some stair-work, some trunk-work, some behind-door-work; they were warmer that got this than the poor thing is here. I'll take it up for pity; yet I'll tarry till my son come; he halloo'd but even now. Whoa-ho-hoa!
Enter Clown

CLOWN: Hilloa, loa!

SHEPHERD: What, art so near? If thou'lt see a thing to talk on when thou art dead and rotten, come hither. What ail'st thou, man?

CLOWN: I have seen two such sights, by sea and by land! But I am not to say it is a sea, for it is now the sky; betwixt the firmament and it you cannot thrust a bodkin's point.

SHEPHERD: Why, boy, how is it?

CLOWN: I would you did but see how it chafes, how it rages, how it takes up the shore! But that's not to the point. O, the most piteous cry of the poor souls! Sometimes to see 'em, and not to see 'em; now the ship boring the moon with her mainmast, and anon swallowed with yeast and froth, as you'd thrust a cork into a hogshead. And then for the land service- to see how the bear tore out his shoulder-bone; how he cried to me for help, and said his name was Antigonus, a nobleman! But to make an end of the ship- to see how the sea flap-dragon'd it; but first, how the poor souls roared, and the sea mock'd them; and how the poor gentleman roared, and the bear mock'd him, both roaring louder than the sea or weather.

SHEPHERD: Name of mercy, when was this, boy?

CLOWN: Now, now; I have not wink'd since I saw these sights; the men are not yet cold under water, nor the bear half din'd on the gentleman; he's at it now.

SHEPHERD: Would I had been by to have help'd the old man!

CLOWN: I would you had been by the ship-side, to have help'd her; there your charity would have lack'd footing.

SHEPHERD: Heavy matters, heavy matters! But look thee here, boy. Now bless thyself; thou met'st with things dying, I with things new-born. Here's a sight for thee; look thee, a bearing-cloth for a squire's child! Look thee here; take up, take up, boy; open't. So, let's see- it was told me I should be rich by the fairies. This is some changeling. Open't. What's within, boy?

CLOWN: You're a made old man; if the sins of your youth are forgiven you, you're well to live. Gold! all gold!

SHEPHERD: This is fairy gold, boy, and 'twill prove so. Up with't, keep it close. Home, home, the next way! We are lucky, boy; and to be so still requires nothing but secrecy. Let my sheep go. Come, good boy, the next way home.

CLOWN: Go you the next way with your findings. I'll go see if the bear be gone from the gentleman, and how much he hath eaten. They are never curst but when they are hungry. If there be any of him left, I'll bury it.

SHEPHERD: That's a good deed. If thou mayest discern by that which is left of him what he is, fetch me to th' sight of him.

CLOWN: Marry, will I; and you shall help to put him i' th' ground.

SHEPHERD: 'Tis a lucky day, boy; and we'll do good deeds on't.
Exeunt

ACT IV. SCENE I. Enter Time, the Chorus

TIME: I, that please some, try all, both joy and terror
Of good and bad, that makes and unfolds error,
Now take upon me, in the name of Time,
To use my wings. Impute it not a crime
To me or my swift passage that I slide
O'er sixteen years, and leave the growth untried
Of that wide gap, since it is in my pow'r
To o'erthrow law, and in one self-born hour
To plant and o'erwhelm custom. Let me pass
The same I am, ere ancient'st order was
Or what is now receiv'd. I witness to
The times that brought them in; so shall I do
To th' freshest things now reigning, and make stale
The glistering of this present, as my tale
Now seems to it. Your patience this allowing,
I turn my glass, and give my scene such growing
As you had slept between. Leontes leaving-
Th' effects of his fond jealousies so grieving

That he shuts up himself- imagine me,
Gentle spectators, that I now may be
In fair Bohemia; and remember well
I mention'd a son o' th' King's, which Florizel
I now name to you; and with speed so pace
To speak of Perdita, now grown in grace
Equal with wond'ring. What of her ensues
I list not prophesy; but let Time's news
Be known when 'tis brought forth. A shepherd's daughter,
And what to her adheres, which follows after,
Is th' argument of Time. Of this allow,
If ever you have spent time worse ere now;
If never, yet that Time himself doth say
He wishes earnestly you never may.
  Exit

ACT IV. SCENE II. Bohemia. The Palace of Polixenes
Enter Polixenes and Camillo

POLIXENES: I pray thee, good Camillo, be no more importunate: 'tis a sickness denying thee anything; a death to grant this.

CAMILLO: It is fifteen years since I saw my country; though I have for the most part been aired abroad, I desire to lay my bones there. Besides, the penitent King, my master, hath sent for me; to whose feeling sorrows I might be some allay, or I o'erween to think so, which is another spur to my departure.

POLIXENES: As thou lov'st me, Camillo, wipe not out the rest of thy services by leaving me now. The need I have of thee thine own goodness hath made. Better not to have had thee than thus to want thee; thou, having made me businesses which none without thee can sufficiently manage, must either stay to execute them thyself, or take away with thee the very services thou hast done; which if I have not enough considered- as too much I cannot- to be more thankful to thee shall be my study; and my profit therein the heaping friendships. Of that fatal country Sicilia, prithee, speak no more; whose very naming punishes me with the remembrance of that penitent, as thou call'st him, and reconciled king, my brother; whose loss of his most precious queen and children are even now to be afresh lamented. Say to me, when saw'st thou the Prince Florizel, my son? Kings are no less unhappy, their issue not being gracious, than they are in losing them when they have approved their virtues.

CAMILLO: Sir, it is three days since I saw the Prince. What his happier affairs may be are to me unknown; but I have missingly noted he is of late much retired from court, and is less frequent to his princely exercises than formerly he hath appeared.

POLIXENES: I have considered so much, Camillo, and with some care, so far that I have eyes under my service which look upon his removedness; from whom I have this intelligence, that he is seldom from the house of a most homely shepherd- a man, they say, that from very nothing, and beyond the imagination of his neighbours, is grown into an unspeakable estate.

CAMILLO: I have heard, sir, of such a man, who hath a daughter of most rare note. The report of her is extended more than can be thought to begin from such a cottage.

POLIXENES: That's likewise part of my intelligence; but, I fear, the angle that plucks our son thither. Thou shalt accompany us to the place; where we will, not appearing what we are, have some question with the shepherd; from whose simplicity I think it not uneasy to get the cause of my son's resort thither. Prithee be my present partner in this business, and lay aside the thoughts of Sicilia.

CAMILLO: I willingly obey your command.

POLIXENES: My best Camillo! We must disguise ourselves.
Exeunt

ACT IV. SCENE III. Bohemia. A Road near the Shepherd's Cottage
Enter Autolycus, Singing
When daffodils begin to peer,
  With heigh! the doxy over the dale,

Why, then comes in the sweet o' the year,
  For the red blood reigns in the winter's pale.

The white sheet bleaching on the hedge,
  With heigh! the sweet birds, O, how they sing!
Doth set my pugging tooth on edge,
  For a quart of ale is a dish for a king.

The lark, that tirra-lirra chants,
  With heigh! with heigh! the thrush and the jay,
Are summer songs for me and my aunts,
  While we lie tumbling in the hay.

I have serv'd Prince Florizel, and in my time wore three-pile;
but now I am out of service.

But shall I go mourn for that, my dear?
  The pale moon shines by night;
And when I wander here and there,
  I then do most go right.

If tinkers may have leave to live,
  And bear the sow-skin budget,
Then my account I well may give
  And in the stocks avouch it.

My traffic is sheets; when the kite builds, look to lesser linen. My father
nam'd me Autolycus; who, being, I as am, litter'd under Mercury, was
likewise a snapper-up of unconsidered trifles. With die and drab I purchas'd
this caparison; and my revenue is the silly-cheat. Gallows and knock are too
powerful on the highway; beating and hanging are terrors to me; for the life
to come, Isleep out the thought of it. A prize! a prize!
  Enter Clown

CLOWN: Let me see: every 'leven wether tods; every tod yields pound and
odd shilling; fifteen hundred shorn, what comes the wool to?

AUTOLYCUS: *Aside* If the springe hold, the cock's mine.

CLOWN: I cannot do 't without counters. Let me see: what am I to buy for our sheep-shearing feast? Three pound of sugar, five pound of currants, rice-what will this sister of mine do with rice? But my father hath made her mistress of the feast, and she lays it on. She hath made me four and twenty nosegays for the shearers- three-man song-men all, and very good ones; but they are most of them means and bases; but one Puritan amongst them, and he sings psalms to hornpipes. I must have saffron to colour the warden pies; mace; dates- none, that's out of my note; nutmegs, seven; race or two of ginger, but that I may beg; four pound of prunes, and as many of raisins o' th' sun.

AUTOLYCUS: *Grovelling on the Ground* O that ever I was born!

CLOWN: I' th' name of me!

AUTOLYCUS: O, help me, help me! Pluck but off these rags; and then, death, death!

CLOWN: Alack, poor soul! thou hast need of more rags to lay on thee, rather than have these off.

AUTOLYCUS: O sir, the loathsomeness of them offend me more than the stripes I have received, which are mighty ones and millions.

CLOWN: Alas, poor man! a million of beating may come to a great matter.

AUTOLYCUS: I am robb'd, sir, and beaten; my money and apparel ta'en from me, and these detestable things put upon me.

CLOWN: What, by a horseman or a footman?

AUTOLYCUS: A footman, sweet sir, a footman.

CLOWN: Indeed, he should be a footman, by the garments he has left with thee; if this be a horseman's coat, it hath seen very hot service. Lend me thy hand, I'll help thee. Come, lend me thy hand. *Helping Him Up*

AUTOLYCUS: O, good sir, tenderly, O!

CLOWN: Alas, poor soul!

AUTOLYCUS: O, good sir, softly, good sir; I fear, sir, my shoulder blade is out.

CLOWN: How now! Canst stand?

AUTOLYCUS: Softly, dear sir *Picks His Pocket*; good sir, softly. You ha' done me a charitable office.

CLOWN: Dost lack any money? I have a little money for thee.

AUTOLYCUS: No, good sweet sir; no, I beseech you, sir. I have a kinsman not past three quarters of a mile hence, unto whom I was going; I shall there have money or anything I want. Offer me no money, I pray you; that kills my heart.

CLOWN: What manner of fellow was he that robb'd you?

AUTOLYCUS: A fellow, sir, that I have known to go about with troll-my-dames; I knew him once a servant of the Prince. I cannot tell, good sir, for which of his virtues it was, but he was certainly whipt out of the court.

CLOWN: His vices, you would say; there's no virtue whipt out of the court. They cherish it to make it stay there; and yet it will no more but abide.

AUTOLYCUS: Vices, I would say, sir. I know this man well; he hath been since an ape-bearer; then a process-server, a bailiff; then he compass'd a motion of the Prodigal Son, and married a tinker's wife within a mile where my land and living lies; and, having flown over many knavish professions, he settled only in rogue. Some call him Autolycus.

CLOWN: Out upon him! prig, for my life, prig! He haunts wakes, fairs, and bear-baitings.

AUTOLYCUS: Very true, sir; he, sir, he; that's the rogue that put me into this apparel.

CLOWN: Not a more cowardly rogue in all Bohemia; if you had but look'd big and spit at him, he'd have run.

AUTOLYCUS: I must confess to you, sir, I am no fighter; I am false of heart that way, and that he knew, I warrant him.

CLOWN: How do you now?

AUTOLYCUS: Sweet sir, much better than I was; I can stand and walk. I will even take my leave of you and pace softly towards my kinsman's.

CLOWN: Shall I bring thee on the way?

AUTOLYCUS: No, good-fac'd sir; no, sweet sir.

CLOWN: Then fare thee well. I must go buy spices for our sheep-shearing.

AUTOLYCUS: Prosper you, sweet sir!
Exit Clown
Your purse is not hot enough to purchase your spice. I'll be with you at your sheep-shearing too. If I make not this cheat bring out another, and the shearers prove sheep, let me be unroll'd, and my name put in the book of virtue!
Sings
Jog on, jog on, the footpath way,
    And merrily hent the stile-a;
A merry heart goes all the day,
    Your sad tires in a mile-a. *Exit*

ACT IV. SCENE IV. Bohemia. The Shepherd's Cottage

Enter Florizel and Perdita

FLORIZEL: These your unusual weeds to each part of you
Do give a life- no shepherdess, but Flora
Peering in April's front. This your sheep-shearing
Is as a meeting of the petty gods,
And you the Queen on't.

PERDITA: Sir, my gracious lord,
To chide at your extremes it not becomes me-
O, pardon that I name them! Your high self,
The gracious mark o' th' land, you have obscur'd
With a swain's wearing; and me, poor lowly maid,
Most goddess-like prank'd up. But that our feasts
In every mess have folly, and the feeders
Digest it with a custom, I should blush
To see you so attir'd; swoon, I think,
To show myself a glass.

FLORIZEL: I bless the time
When my good falcon made her flight across
Thy father's ground.

PERDITA: Now Jove afford you cause!
To me the difference forges dread; your greatness
Hath not been us'd to fear. Even now I tremble
To think your father, by some accident,
Should pass this way, as you did. O, the Fates!
How would he look to see his work, so noble,
Vilely bound up? What would he say? Or how
Should I, in these my borrowed flaunts, behold
The sternness of his presence?

FLORIZEL: Apprehend
Nothing but jollity. The gods themselves,
Humbling their deities to love, have taken

The shapes of beasts upon them: Jupiter
Became a bull and bellow'd; the green Neptune
A ram and bleated; and the fire-rob'd god,
Golden Apollo, a poor humble swain,
As I seem now. Their transformations
Were never for a piece of beauty rarer,
Nor in a way so chaste, since my desires
Run not before mine honour, nor my lusts
Burn hotter than my faith.

PERDITA: O, but, sir,
Your resolution cannot hold when 'tis
Oppos'd, as it must be, by th' pow'r of the King.
One of these two must be necessities,
Which then will speak, that you must change this purpose,
Or I my life.

FLORIZEL: Thou dearest Perdita,
With these forc'd thoughts, I prithee, darken not
The mirth o' th' feast. Or I'll be thine, my fair,
Or not my father's; for I cannot be
Mine own, nor anything to any, if
I be not thine. To this I am most constant,
Though destiny say no. Be merry, gentle;
Strangle such thoughts as these with any thing
That you behold the while. Your guests are coming.
Lift up your countenance, as it were the day
Of celebration of that nuptial which
We two have sworn shall come.

PERDITA: O Lady Fortune,
Stand you auspicious!

FLORIZEL: See, your guests approach.
Address yourself to entertain them sprightly,
And let's be red with mirth.

Enter Shepherd, with Polixenes and Camillo, Disguised; Clown, Mopsa, Dorcas, with Others

SHEPHERD: Fie, daughter! When my old wife liv'd, upon
This day she was both pantler, butler, cook;
Both dame and servant; welcom'd all; serv'd all;
Would sing her song and dance her turn; now here
At upper end o' th' table, now i' th' middle;
On his shoulder, and his; her face o' fire
With labour, and the thing she took to quench it
She would to each one sip. You are retired,
As if you were a feasted one, and not
The hostess of the meeting. Pray you bid
These unknown friends to's welcome, for it is
A way to make us better friends, more known.
Come, quench your blushes, and present yourself
That which you are, Mistress o' th' Feast. Come on,
And bid us welcome to your sheep-shearing,
As your good flock shall prosper.

PERDITA: *To Polixenes* Sir, welcome.
It is my father's will I should take on me
The hostess-ship o' th' day.
To Camillo You're welcome, sir.
Give me those flow'rs there, Dorcas. Reverend sirs,
For you there's rosemary and rue; these keep
Seeming and savour all the winter long.
Grace and remembrance be to you both!
And welcome to our shearing.

POLIXENES: Shepherdess-
A fair one are you- well you fit our ages
With flow'rs of winter.

PERDITA: Sir, the year growing ancient,
Not yet on summer's death nor on the birth
Of trembling winter, the fairest flow'rs o' th' season

Are our carnations and streak'd gillyvors,
Which some call nature's bastards. Of that kind
Our rustic garden's barren; and I care not
To get slips of them.

POLIXENES: Wherefore, gentle maiden,
Do you neglect them?

PERDITA: For I have heard it said
There is an art which in their piedness shares
With great creating nature.

POLIXENES: Say there be;
Yet nature is made better by no mean
But nature makes that mean; so over that art
Which you say adds to nature, is an art
That nature makes. You see, sweet maid, we marry
A gentler scion to the wildest stock,
And make conceive a bark of baser kind
By bud of nobler race. This is an art
Which does mend nature- change it rather; but
The art itself is nature.

PERDITA: So it is.

POLIXENES: Then make your garden rich in gillyvors,
And do not call them bastards.

PERDITA: I'll not put
The dibble in earth to set one slip of them;
No more than were I painted I would wish
This youth should say 'twere well, and only therefore
Desire to breed by me. Here's flow'rs for you:
Hot lavender, mints, savory, marjoram;
The marigold, that goes to bed wi' th' sun,
And with him rises weeping; these are flow'rs
Of middle summer, and I think they are given

To men of middle age. Y'are very welcome.

CAMILLO: I should leave grazing, were I of your flock,
And only live by gazing.

PERDITA: Out, alas!
You'd be so lean that blasts of January
Would blow you through and through. Now, my fair'st friend,
I would I had some flow'rs o' th' spring that might
Become your time of day- and yours, and yours,
That wear upon your virgin branches yet
Your maidenheads growing. O Proserpina,
From the flowers now that, frighted, thou let'st fall
From Dis's waggon!- daffodils,
That come before the swallow dares, and take
The winds of March with beauty; violets, dim
But sweeter than the lids of Juno's eyes
Or Cytherea's breath; pale primroses,
That die unmarried ere they can behold
Bright Phoebus in his strength- a malady
Most incident to maids; bold oxlips, and
The crown-imperial; lilies of all kinds,
The flow'r-de-luce being one. O, these I lack
To make you garlands of, and my sweet friend
To strew him o'er and o'er!

FLORIZEL: What, like a corse?

PERDITA: No; like a bank for love to lie and play on;
Not like a corse; or if- not to be buried,
But quick, and in mine arms. Come, take your flow'rs.
Methinks I play as I have seen them do
In Whitsun pastorals. Sure, this robe of mine
Does change my disposition.

FLORIZEL: What you do
Still betters what is done. When you speak, sweet,

I'd have you do it ever. When you sing,
I'd have you buy and sell so; so give alms;
Pray so; and, for the ord'ring your affairs,
To sing them too. When you do dance, I wish you
A wave o' th' sea, that you might ever do
Nothing but that; move still, still so,
And own no other function. Each your doing,
So singular in each particular,
Crowns what you are doing in the present deeds,
That all your acts are queens.

PERDITA: O Doricles,
Your praises are too large. But that your youth,
And the true blood which peeps fairly through't,
Do plainly give you out an unstain'd shepherd,
With wisdom I might fear, my Doricles,
You woo'd me the false way.

FLORIZEL: I think you have
As little skill to fear as I have purpose
To put you to't. But, come; our dance, I pray.
Your hand, my Perdita; so turtles pair
That never mean to part.

PERDITA: I'll swear for 'em.

POLIXENES: This is the prettiest low-born lass that ever
Ran on the green-sward; nothing she does or seems
But smacks of something greater than herself,
Too noble for this place.

CAMILLO: He tells her something
That makes her blood look out. Good sooth, she is
The queen of curds and cream.

CLOWN: Come on, strike up.

DORCAS: Mopsa must be your mistress; marry, garlic,
To mend her kissing with!

MOPSA: Now, in good time!

CLOWN: Not a word, a word; we stand upon our manners.
Come, strike up. *Music*
  Here a Dance of Shepherds and Shepherdesses

POLIXENES: Pray, good shepherd, what fair swain is this
Which dances with your daughter?

SHEPHERD: They call him Doricles, and boasts himself
To have a worthy feeding; but I have it
Upon his own report, and I believe it:
He looks like sooth. He says he loves my daughter;
I think so too; for never gaz'd the moon
Upon the water as he'll stand and read,
As 'twere my daughter's eyes; and, to be plain,
I think there is not half a kiss to choose
Who loves another best.

POLIXENES: She dances featly.

SHEPHERD: So she does any thing; though I report it
That should be silent. If young Doricles
Do light upon her, she shall bring him that
Which he not dreams of.
  Enter a Servant

SERVANT: O master, if you did but hear the pedlar at the door, you would
never dance again after a tabor and pipe; no, the bagpipe could not move
you. He sings several tunes faster than you'll tell money; he utters them as he
had eaten ballads, and all men's ears grew to his tunes.

CLOWN: He could never come better; he shall come in. I love a ballad but even too well, if it be doleful matter merrily set down, or a very pleasant thing indeed and sung lamentably.

SERVANT: He hath songs for man or woman of all sizes; no milliner can so fit his customers with gloves. He has the prettiest love-songs for maids; so without bawdry, which is strange; with such delicate burdens of dildos and fadings, 'jump her and thump her'; and where some stretch-mouth'd rascal would, as it were, mean mischief, and break a foul gap into the matter, he makes the maid to answer 'Whoop, do me no harm, good man'- puts him off, slights him, with 'Whoop, do me no harm, good man.'

POLIXENES: This is a brave fellow.

CLOWN: Believe me, thou talkest of an admirable conceited fellow. Has he any unbraided wares?

SERVANT: He hath ribbons of all the colours i' th' rainbow; points, more than all the lawyers in Bohemia can learnedly handle, though they come to him by th' gross; inkles, caddisses, cambrics, lawns. Why he sings 'em over as they were gods or goddesses; you would think a smock were she-angel, he so chants to the sleeve-hand and the work about the square on't.

CLOWN: Prithee bring him in; and let him approach singing.

PERDITA: Forewarn him that he use no scurrilous words in's tunes.
  Exit Servant

CLOWN: You have of these pedlars that have more in them than you'd think, sister.

PERDITA: Ay, good brother, or go about to think.
  Enter Autolycus, Singing
      Lawn as white as driven snow;
      Cypress black as e'er was crow;
      Gloves as sweet as damask roses;
      Masks for faces and for noses;

Bugle bracelet, necklace amber,
Perfume for a lady's chamber;
Golden quoifs and stomachers,
For my lads to give their dears;
Pins and poking-sticks of steel-
What maids lack from head to heel.
Come, buy of me, come; come buy, come buy;
Buy, lads, or else your lasses cry.
Come, buy.

CLOWN: If I were not in love with Mopsa, thou shouldst take no money of me; but being enthrall'd as I am, it will also be the bondage of certain ribbons and gloves.

MOPSA: I was promis'd them against the feast; but they come not too late now.

DORCAS: He hath promis'd you more than that, or there be liars.

MOPSA: He hath paid you all he promis'd you. May be he has paid you more, which will shame you to give him again.

CLOWN: Is there no manners left among maids? Will they wear their plackets where they should bear their faces? Is there not milking-time, when you are going to bed, or kiln-hole, to whistle off these secrets, but you must be tittle-tattling before all our guests? 'Tis well they are whisp'ring. Clammer your tongues, and not a word more.

MOPSA: I have done. Come, you promis'd me a tawdry-lace, and a pair of sweet gloves.

CLOWN: Have I not told thee how I was cozen'd by the way, and lost all my money?

AUTOLYCUS: And indeed, sir, there are cozeners abroad; therefore it behoves men to be wary.

CLOWN: Fear not thou, man; thou shalt lose nothing here.

AUTOLYCUS: I hope so, sir; for I have about me many parcels of charge.

CLOWN: What hast here? Ballads?

MOPSA: Pray now, buy some. I love a ballad in print a-life, for then we are sure they are true.

AUTOLYCUS: Here's one to a very doleful tune: how a usurer's wife was brought to bed of twenty money-bags at a burden, and how she long'd to eat adders' heads and toads carbonado'd.

MOPSA: Is it true, think you?

AUTOLYCUS: Very true, and but a month old.

DORCAS: Bless me from marrying a usurer!

AUTOLYCUS: Here's the midwife's name to't, one Mistress Taleporter, and five or six honest wives that were present. Why should I carry lies abroad?

MOPSA: Pray you now, buy it.

CLOWN: Come on, lay it by; and let's first see moe ballads; we'll buy the other things anon.

AUTOLYCUS: Here's another ballad, of a fish that appeared upon the coast on Wednesday the fourscore of April, forty thousand fathom above water, and sung this ballad against the hard hearts of maids. It was thought she was a woman, and was turn'd into a cold fish for she would not exchange flesh with one that lov'd her. The ballad is very pitiful, and as true.

DORCAS: Is it true too, think you?

AUTOLYCUS: Five justices' hands at it; and witnesses more than my pack will hold.

CLOWN: Lay it by too. Another.

AUTOLYCUS: This is a merry ballad, but a very pretty one.

MOPSA: Let's have some merry ones.

AUTOLYCUS: Why, this is a passing merry one, and goes to the tune of 'Two maids wooing a man.' There's scarce a maid westward but she sings it; 'tis in request, I can tell you.

MOPSA: can both sing it. If thou'lt bear a part, thou shalt hear; 'tis in three parts.

DORCAS: We had the tune on't a month ago.

AUTOLYCUS: I can bear my part; you must know 'tis my occupation. Have at it with you.
   Song

AUTOLYCUS: Get you hence, for I must go
       Where it fits not you to know.

DORCAS: Whither?

MOPSA: O, whither?

DORCAS: Whither?

MOPSA: It becomes thy oath full well
       Thou to me thy secrets tell.

DORCAS: Me too! Let me go thither

MOPSA: Or thou goest to th' grange or mill.

DORCAS: If to either, thou dost ill.

AUTOLYCUS: Neither.

DORCAS: What, neither?

AUTOLYCUS: Neither.

DORCAS: Thou hast sworn my love to be.

MOPSA: Thou hast sworn it more to me.
Then whither goest? Say, whither?

CLOWN: We'll have this song out anon by ourselves; my father and the gentlemen are in sad talk, and we'll not trouble them. Come, bring away thy pack after me. Wenches, I'll buy for you both. Pedlar, let's have the first choice. Follow me, girls.
Exit with Dorcas and Mopsa

AUTOLYCUS: And you shall pay well for 'em.
Exit Autolycus, Singing

> Will you buy any tape,
>   Or lace for your cape,
> My dainty duck, my dear-a?
>   Any silk, any thread,
>   Any toys for your head,
> Of the new'st and fin'st, fin'st wear-a?
>   Come to the pedlar;
>   Money's a meddler
> That doth utter all men's ware-a.
Re-enter Servant

SERVANT: Master, there is three carters, three shepherds, three neat-herds, three swineherds, that have made themselves all men of hair; they call themselves Saltiers, and they have dance which the wenches say is a gallimaufry of gambols, because they are not in't; but they themselves are o' th' mind, if it be not too rough for some that know little but bowling, it will please plentifully.

SHEPHERD: Away! We'll none on't; here has been too much homely foolery already. I know, sir, we weary you.

POLIXENES: You weary those that refresh us. Pray, let's see these four threes of herdsmen.

SERVANT: One three of them, by their own report, sir, hath danc'd before the King; and not the worst of the three but jumps twelve foot and a half by th' squier.

SHEPHERD: Leave your prating; since these good men are pleas'd, let them come in; but quickly now.

SERVANT: Why, they stay at door, sir.
Exit
Here a Dance of Twelve Satyrs

POLIXENES: *To Shepherd* O, father, you'll know more of that hereafter.
To Camillo Is it not too far gone? 'Tis time to part them.
He's simple and tells much. *To Florizel* How now, fair shepherd!
Your heart is full of something that does take
Your mind from feasting. Sooth, when I was young
And handed love as you do, I was wont
To load my she with knacks; I would have ransack'd
The pedlar's silken treasury and have pour'd it
To her acceptance: you have let him go
And nothing marted with him. If your lass
Interpretation should abuse and call this
Your lack of love or bounty, you were straited
For a reply, at least if you make a care
Of happy holding her.

FLORIZEL: Old sir, I know
She prizes not such trifles as these are.
The gifts she looks from me are pack'd and lock'd
Up in my heart, which I have given already,
But not deliver'd. O, hear me breathe my life

Before this ancient sir, whom, it should seem,
Hath sometime lov'd. I take thy hand- this hand,
As soft as dove's down and as white as it,
Or Ethiopian's tooth, or the fann'd snow that's bolted
By th' northern blasts twice o'er.

POLIXENES: What follows this?
How prettily the young swain seems to wash
The hand was fair before! I have put you out.
But to your protestation; let me hear
What you profess.

FLORIZEL: Do, and be witness to't.

POLIXENES: And this my neighbour too?

FLORIZEL: And he, and more
Than he, and men- the earth, the heavens, and all:
That, were I crown'd the most imperial monarch,
Thereof most worthy, were I the fairest youth
That ever made eye swerve, had force and knowledge
More than was ever man's, I would not prize them
Without her love; for her employ them all;
Commend them and condemn them to her service
Or to their own perdition.

POLIXENES: Fairly offer'd.

CAMILLO: This shows a sound affection.

SHEPHERD: But, my daughter,
Say you the like to him?

PERDITA: I cannot speak
So well, nothing so well; no, nor mean better.
By th' pattern of mine own thoughts I cut out
The purity of his.

SHEPHERD: Take hands, a bargain!
And, friends unknown, you shall bear witness to't:
I give my daughter to him, and will make
Her portion equal his.

FLORIZEL: O, that must be
I' th' virtue of your daughter. One being dead,
I shall have more than you can dream of yet;
Enough then for your wonder. But come on,
Contract us fore these witnesses.

SHEPHERD: Come, your hand;
And, daughter, yours.

POLIXENES: Soft, swain, awhile, beseech you;
Have you a father?

FLORIZEL: I have, but what of him?

POLIXENES: Knows he of this?

FLORIZEL: He neither does nor shall.

POLIXENES: Methinks a father
Is at the nuptial of his son a guest
That best becomes the table. Pray you, once more,
Is not your father grown incapable
Of reasonable affairs? Is he not stupid
With age and alt'ring rheums? Can he speak, hear,
Know man from man, dispute his own estate?
Lies he not bed-rid, and again does nothing
But what he did being childish?

FLORIZEL: No, good sir;
He has his health, and ampler strength indeed
Than most have of his age.

POLIXENES: By my white beard,
You offer him, if this be so, a wrong
Something unfilial. Reason my son
Should choose himself a wife; but as good reason
The father- all whose joy is nothing else
But fair posterity- should hold some counsel
In such a business.

FLORIZEL: I yield all this;
But, for some other reasons, my grave sir,
Which 'tis not fit you know, I not acquaint
My father of this business.

POLIXENES: Let him know't.

FLORIZEL: He shall not.

POLIXENES: Prithee let him.

FLORIZEL: No, he must not.

SHEPHERD: Let him, my son; he shall not need to grieve
At knowing of thy choice.

FLORIZEL: Come, come, he must not.
Mark our contract.

POLIXENES: *Discovering Himself* Mark your divorce, young sir,
Whom son I dare not call; thou art too base
To be acknowledg'd- thou a sceptre's heir,
That thus affects a sheep-hook! Thou, old traitor,
I am sorry that by hanging thee I can but
Shorten thy life one week. And thou, fresh piece
Of excellent witchcraft, who of force must know
The royal fool thou cop'st with-

SHEPHERD: O, my heart!

POLIXENES: I'll have thy beauty scratch'd with briers and made
More homely than thy state. For thee, fond boy,
If I may ever know thou dost but sigh
That thou no more shalt see this knack- as never
I mean thou shalt- we'll bar thee from succession;
Not hold thee of our blood, no, not our kin,
Farre than Deucalion off. Mark thou my words.
Follow us to the court. Thou churl, for this time,
Though full of our displeasure, yet we free thee
From the dead blow of it. And you, enchantment,
Worthy enough a herdsman- yea, him too
That makes himself, but for our honour therein,
Unworthy thee- if ever henceforth thou
These rural latches to his entrance open,
Or hoop his body more with thy embraces,
I will devise a death as cruel for thee
As thou art tender to't.
   Exit

PERDITA: Even here undone!
I was not much afeard; for once or twice
I was about to speak and tell him plainly
The self-same sun that shines upon his court
Hides not his visage from our cottage, but
Looks on alike. *To Florizel* Will't please you, sir, be gone?
I told you what would come of this. Beseech you,
Of your own state take care. This dream of mine-
Being now awake, I'll queen it no inch farther,
But milk my ewes and weep.

CAMILLO: Why, how now, father!
Speak ere thou diest.

SHEPHERD: I cannot speak nor think,
Nor dare to know that which I know.
To Florizel O sir,
You have undone a man of fourscore-three

That thought to fill his grave in quiet, yea,
To die upon the bed my father died,
To lie close by his honest bones; but now
Some hangman must put on my shroud and lay me
Where no priest shovels in dust.
To Perdita O cursed wretch,
That knew'st this was the Prince, and wouldst adventure
To mingle faith with him!- Undone, undone!
If I might die within this hour, I have liv'd
To die when I desire.
    Exit

FLORIZEL: Why look you so upon me?
I am but sorry, not afeard; delay'd,
But nothing alt'red. What I was, I am:
More straining on for plucking back; not following
My leash unwillingly.

CAMILLO: Gracious, my lord,
You know your father's temper. At this time
He will allow no speech- which I do guess
You do not purpose to him- and as hardly
Will he endure your sight as yet, I fear;
Then, till the fury of his Highness settle,
Come not before him.

FLORIZEL: I not purpose it.
I think Camillo?

CAMILLO: Even he, my lord.

PERDITA: How often have I told you 'twould be thus!
How often said my dignity would last
But till 'twere known!

FLORIZEL: It cannot fail but by
The violation of my faith; and then

Let nature crush the sides o' th' earth together
And mar the seeds within! Lift up thy looks.
From my succession wipe me, father; I
Am heir to my affection.

CAMILLO: Be advis'd.

FLORIZEL: I am- and by my fancy; if my reason
Will thereto be obedient, I have reason;
If not, my senses, better pleas'd with madness,
Do bid it welcome.

CAMILLO: This is desperate, sir.

FLORIZEL: So call it; but it does fulfil my vow:
I needs must think it honesty. Camillo,
Not for Bohemia, nor the pomp that may
Be thereat glean'd, for all the sun sees or
The close earth wombs, or the profound seas hides
In unknown fathoms, will I break my oath
To this my fair belov'd. Therefore, I pray you,
As you have ever been my father's honour'd friend,
When he shall miss me- as, in faith, I mean not
To see him any more- cast your good counsels
Upon his passion. Let myself and Fortune
Tug for the time to come. This you may know,
And so deliver: I am put to sea
With her who here I cannot hold on shore.
And most opportune to her need I have
A vessel rides fast by, but not prepar'd
For this design. What course I mean to hold
Shall nothing benefit your knowledge, nor
Concern me the reporting.

CAMILLO: O my lord,
I would your spirit were easier for advice.
Or stronger for your need.

FLORIZEL: Hark, Perdita. *Takes Her Aside*
To Camillo I'll hear you by and by.

CAMILLO: He's irremovable,
Resolv'd for flight. Now were I happy if
His going I could frame to serve my turn,
Save him from danger, do him love and honour,
Purchase the sight again of dear Sicilia
And that unhappy king, my master, whom
I so much thirst to see.

FLORIZEL: Now, good Camillo,
I am so fraught with curious business that
I leave out ceremony.

CAMILLO: Sir, I think
You have heard of my poor services i' th' love
That I have borne your father?

FLORIZEL: Very nobly
Have you deserv'd. It is my father's music
To speak your deeds; not little of his care
To have them recompens'd as thought on.

CAMILLO: Well, my lord,
If you may please to think I love the King,
And through him what's nearest to him, which is
Your gracious self, embrace but my direction.
If your more ponderous and settled project
May suffer alteration, on mine honour,
I'll point you where you shall have such receiving
As shall become your Highness; where you may
Enjoy your mistress, from the whom, I see,
There's no disjunction to be made but by,
As heavens forfend! your ruin- marry her;
And with my best endeavours in your absence
Your discontenting father strive to qualify,

And bring him up to liking.

FLORIZEL: How, Camillo,
May this, almost a miracle, be done?
That I may call thee something more than man,
And after that trust to thee.

CAMILLO: Have you thought on
A place whereto you'll go?

FLORIZEL: Not any yet;
But as th' unthought-on accident is guilty
To what we wildly do, so we profess
Ourselves to be the slaves of chance and flies
Of every wind that blows.

CAMILLO: Then list to me.
This follows, if you will not change your purpose
But undergo this flight: make for Sicilia,
And there present yourself and your fair princess-
For so, I see, she must be- fore Leontes.
She shall be habited as it becomes
The partner of your bed. Methinks I see
Leontes opening his free arms and weeping
His welcomes forth; asks thee there 'Son, forgiveness!'
As 'twere i' th' father's person; kisses the hands
Of your fresh princess; o'er and o'er divides him
'Twixt his unkindness and his kindness- th' one
He chides to hell, and bids the other grow
Faster than thought or time.

FLORIZEL: Worthy Camillo,
What colour for my visitation shall I
Hold up before him?

CAMILLO: Sent by the King your father
To greet him and to give him comforts. Sir,

The manner of your bearing towards him, with
What you as from your father shall deliver,
Things known betwixt us three, I'll write you down;
The which shall point you forth at every sitting
What you must say, that he shall not perceive
But that you have your father's bosom there
And speak his very heart.

FLORIZEL: I am bound to you.
There is some sap in this.

CAMILLO: A course more promising
Than a wild dedication of yourselves
To unpath'd waters, undream'd shores, most certain
To miseries enough; no hope to help you,
But as you shake off one to take another;
Nothing so certain as your anchors, who
Do their best office if they can but stay you
Where you'll be loath to be. Besides, you know
Prosperity's the very bond of love,
Whose fresh complexion and whose heart together
Affliction alters.

PERDITA: One of these is true:
I think affliction may subdue the cheek,
But not take in the mind.

CAMILLO: Yea, say you so?
There shall not at your father's house these seven years
Be born another such.

FLORIZEL: My good Camillo,
She is as forward of her breeding as
She is i' th' rear o' our birth.

CAMILLO: I cannot say 'tis pity
She lacks instructions, for she seems a mistress

To most that teach.

PERDITA: Your pardon, sir; for this
I'll blush you thanks.

FLORIZEL: My prettiest Perdita!
But, O, the thorns we stand upon! Camillo-
Preserver of my father, now of me;
The medicine of our house- how shall we do?
We are not furnish'd like Bohemia's son;
Nor shall appear in Sicilia.

CAMILLO: My lord,
Fear none of this. I think you know my fortunes
Do all lie there. It shall be so my care
To have you royally appointed as if
The scene you play were mine. For instance, sir,
That you may know you shall not want- one word.
   They Talk Aside
   Re-enter Autolycus

AUTOLYCUS: Ha, ha! what a fool Honesty is! and Trust, his sworn
brother, a very simple gentleman! I have sold all my trumpery; not a
counterfeit stone, not a ribbon, glass, pomander, brooch, table-book, ballad,
knife, tape, glove, shoe-tie, bracelet, horn-ring, to keep my pack from fasting.
They throng who should buy first, as if my trinkets had been hallowed and
brought a benediction to the buyer; by which means I saw whose purse was
best in picture; and what I saw, to my good use I rememb'red. My clown,
who wants but something to be a reasonable man, grew so in love with the
wenches' song that he would not stir his pettitoes till he had both tune and
words, which so drew the rest of the herd to me that all their other senses
stuck in ears. You might have pinch'd a placket, it was senseless; 'twas
nothing to geld a codpiece of a purse; I would have fil'd keys off that hung
in chains. No hearing, no feeling, but my sir's song, and admiring the
nothing of it. So that in this time of lethargy I pick'd and cut most of their
festival purses; and had not the old man come in with whoobub against his

daughter and the King's son and scar'd my choughs from the chaff, I had not left a purse alive in the whole army.

Camillo, Florizel, and Perdita Come Forward

CAMILLO: Nay, but my letters, by this means being there So soon as you arrive, shall clear that doubt.

FLORIZEL: And those that you'll procure from King Leontes?

CAMILLO: Shall satisfy your father.

PERDITA: Happy be you!
All that you speak shows fair.

CAMILLO: *Seeing Autolycus* Who have we here?
We'll make an instrument of this; omit
Nothing may give us aid.

AUTOLYCUS: *Aside* If they have overheard me now- why, hanging.

CAMILLO: How now, good fellow! Why shak'st thou so?
Fear not, man; here's no harm intended to thee.

AUTOLYCUS: I am a poor fellow, sir.

CAMILLO: Why, be so still; here's nobody will steal that from thee. Yet for the outside of thy poverty we must make an exchange; therefore discase thee instantly- thou must think there's a necessity in't- and change garments with this gentleman. Though the pennyworth on his side be the worst, yet hold thee, there's some boot. *Giving Money*

AUTOLYCUS: I am a poor fellow, sir. *Aside* I know ye well enough.

CAMILLO: Nay, prithee dispatch. The gentleman is half flay'd already.

AUTOLYCUS: Are you in camest, sir? *Aside* I smell the trick on't.

FLORIZEL: Dispatch, I prithee.

AUTOLYCUS: Indeed, I have had earnest; but I cannot with conscience take it.

CAMILLO: Unbuckle, unbuckle.
   Florizel and Autolycus Exchange Garments
Fortunate mistress- let my prophecy
Come home to ye!- you must retire yourself
Into some covert; take your sweetheart's hat
And pluck it o'er your brows, muffle your face,
Dismantle you, and, as you can, disliken
The truth of your own seeming, that you may-
For I do fear eyes over- to shipboard
Get undescried.

PERDITA: I see the play so lies
That I must bear a part.

CAMILLO: No remedy.
Have you done there?

FLORIZEL: Should I now meet my father,
He would not call me son.

CAMILLO: Nay, you shall have no hat.
   Giving it to Perdita
Come, lady, come. Farewell, my friend.

AUTOLYCUS: Adieu, sir.

FLORIZEL: O Perdita, what have we twain forgot!
Pray you a word. *They Converse Apart*

CAMILLO: *Aside* What I do next shall be to tell the King
Of this escape, and whither they are bound;
Wherein my hope is I shall so prevail

To force him after; in whose company
I shall re-view Sicilia, for whose sight
I have a woman's longing.

FLORIZEL: Fortune speed us!
Thus we set on, Camillo, to th' sea-side.

CAMILLO: The swifter speed the better.
Exeunt Florizel, Perdita, and Camillo

AUTOLYCUS: I understand the business, I hear it. To have an open ear, a quick eye, and a nimble hand, is necessary for a cut-purse; a good nose is requisite also, to smell out work for th' other senses. I see this is the time that the unjust man doth thrive. What an exchange had this been without boot! What a boot is here with this exchange! Sure, the gods do this year connive at us, and we may do anything extempore. The Prince himself is about a piece of iniquity- stealing away from his father with his clog at his heels. If I thought it were a piece of honesty to acquaint the King withal, I would not do't. I hold it the more knavery to conceal it; and therein am I constant to my profession.
Re-enter Clown and Shepherd
Aside, aside- here is more matter for a hot brain. Every lane's end, every shop, church, session, hanging, yields a careful man work.

CLOWN: See, see; what a man you are now! There is no other way but to tell the King she's a changeling and none of your flesh and blood.

SHEPHERD: Nay, but hear me.

DORCAS: Nay- but hear me.

SHEPHERD: Go to, then.

DORCAS: She being none of your flesh and blood, your flesh and blood has not offended the King; and so your flesh and blood is not to be punish'd by him. Show those things you found about her, those secret things- all but what she has with her. This being done, let the law go whistle; I warrant you.

SHEPHERD: I will tell the King all, every word- yea, and his son's pranks too; who, I may say, is no honest man, neither to his father nor to me, to go about to make me the King's brother-in-law.

DORCAS: Indeed, brother-in-law was the farthest off you could have been to him; and then your blood had been the dearer by I know how much an ounce.

AUTOLYCUS: *Aside* Very wisely, puppies!

SHEPHERD: Well, let us to the King. There is that in this fardel will make him scratch his beard.

AUTOLYCUS: *Aside* I know not what impediment this complaint may be to the flight of my master.

DORCAS: Pray heartily he be at palace.

AUTOLYCUS: *Aside* Though I am not naturally honest, I am so sometimes by chance. Let me pocket up my pedlar's excrement. *Takes off His False Beard* How now, rustics! Whither are you bound?

SHEPHERD: To th' palace, an it like your worship.

AUTOLYCUS: Your affairs there, what, with whom, the condition of that fardel, the place of your dwelling, your names, your ages, of what having, breeding, and anything that is fitting to be known- discover.

DORCAS: We are but plain fellows, sir.

AUTOLYCUS: A lie: you are rough and hairy. Let me have no lying; it becomes none but tradesmen, and they often give us soldiers the lie; but we pay them for it with stamped coin, not stabbing steel; therefore they do not give us the lie.

DORCAS: Your worship had like to have given us one, if you had not taken yourself with the manner.

SHEPHERD: Are you a courtier, an't like you, sir?

AUTOLYCUS: Whether it like me or no, I am a courtier. Seest thou not the air of the court in these enfoldings? Hath not my gait in it the measure of the court? Receives not thy nose court-odour from me? Reflect I not on thy baseness court-contempt? Think'st thou, for that I insinuate, that toaze from thee thy business, I am therefore no courtier? I am courtier cap-a-pe, and one that will either push on or pluck back thy business there; whereupon I command the to open thy affair.

SHEPHERD: My business, sir, is to the King.

AUTOLYCUS: What advocate hast thou to him?

SHEPHERD: I know not, an't like you.

DORCAS: Advocate's the court-word for a pheasant; say you have none.

SHEPHERD: None, sir; I have no pheasant, cock nor hen.

AUTOLYCUS: How blessed are we that are not simple men! Yet nature might have made me as these are, Therefore I will not disdain.

DORCAS: This cannot be but a great courtier.

SHEPHERD: His garments are rich, but he wears them not handsomely.

DORCAS: He seems to be the more noble in being fantastical. A great man, I'll warrant; I know by the picking on's teeth.

AUTOLYCUS: The fardel there? What's i' th' fardel? Wherefore that box?

SHEPHERD: Sir, there lies such secrets in this fardel and box which none must know but the King; and which he shall know within this hour, if I may come to th' speech of him.

AUTOLYCUS: Age, thou hast lost thy labour.

SHEPHERD: Why, Sir?

AUTOLYCUS: The King is not at the palace; he is gone aboard a new ship to purge melancholy and air himself; for, if thou be'st capable of things serious, thou must know the King is full of grief.

SHEPHERD: So 'tis said, sir- about his son, that should have married a shepherd's daughter.

AUTOLYCUS: If that shepherd be not in hand-fast, let him fly; the curses he shall have, the tortures he shall feel, will break the back of man, the heart of monster.

DORCAS: Think you so, sir?

AUTOLYCUS: Not he alone shall suffer what wit can make heavy and vengeance bitter; but those that are germane to him, though remov'd fifty times, shall all come under the hangman- which, though it be great pity, yet it is necessary. An old sheep-whistling rogue, a ram-tender, to offer to have his daughter come into grace! Some say he shall be ston'd; but that death is too soft for him, say I. Draw our throne into a sheep-cote!- all deaths are too few, the sharpest too easy.

DORCAS: Has the old man e'er a son, sir, do you hear, an't like you, sir?

AUTOLYCUS: He has a son- who shall be flay'd alive; then 'nointed over with honey, set on the head of a wasp's nest; then stand till he be three quarters and a dram dead; then recover'd again with aqua-vitae or some other hot infusion; then, raw as he is, and in the hottest day prognostication proclaims, shall he be set against a brick wall, the sun looking with a southward eye upon him, where he is to behold him with flies blown to death. But what talk we of these traitorly rascals, whose miseries are to be smil'd at, their offences being so capital? Tell me, for you seem to be honest plain men, what you have to the King. Being something gently consider'd, I'll bring you where he is aboard, tender your persons to his presence, whisper him in your behalfs; and if it be in man besides the King to effect your suits, here is man shall do it.

DORCAS: He seems to be of great authority. Close with him, give him gold; and though authority be a stubborn bear, yet he is oft led by the nose with gold. Show the inside of your purse to the outside of his hand, and no more ado. Remember- ston'd and flay'd alive.

SHEPHERD: An't please you, sir, to undertake the business for us, here is that gold I have. I'll make it as much more, and leave this young man in pawn till I bring it you.

AUTOLYCUS: After I have done what I promised?

SHEPHERD: Ay, sir.

AUTOLYCUS: Well, give me the moiety. Are you a party in this business?

DORCAS: In some sort, sir; but though my case be a pitiful one, I hope I shall not be flay'd out of it.

AUTOLYCUS: O, that's the case of the shepherd's son! Hang him, he'll be made an example.

DORCAS: Comfort, good comfort! We must to the King and show our strange sights. He must know 'tis none of your daughter nor my sister; we are gone else. Sir, I will give you as much as this old man does, when the business is performed; and remain, as he says, your pawn till it be brought you.

AUTOLYCUS: I will trust you. Walk before toward the sea-side; go on the right-hand; I will but look upon the hedge, and follow you.

DORCAS: We are blest in this man, as I may say, even blest.

SHEPHERD: Let's before, as he bids us. He was provided to do us good.

Exeunt Shepherd and Clown Autolycus.

If I had a mind to be honest, I see Fortune would not suffer me: she drops booties in my mouth. I am courted now with a double occasion- gold, and a means to do the Prince my master good; which who knows how that may turn back to my advancement? I will bring these two moles, these blind ones, aboard him. If he think it fit to shore them again, and that the complaint they have to the King concerns him nothing, let him call me rogue for being so far officious; for I am proof against that title, and what shame else belongs to't. To him will I present them. There may be matter in it.

Exit

ACT V. SCENE I. Sicilia. The Palace of Leontes

Enter Leontes, Cleomenes, Dion, Paulina, and Others

CLEOMENES: Sir, you have done enough, and have perform'd
A saint-like sorrow. No fault could you make
Which you have not redeem'd; indeed, paid down
More penitence than done trespass. At the last,
Do as the heavens have done: forget your evil;
With them forgive yourself.

LEONTES: Whilst I remember
Her and her virtues, I cannot forget
My blemishes in them, and so still think of
The wrong I did myself; which was so much
That heirless it hath made my kingdom, and
Destroy'd the sweet'st companion that e'er man
Bred his hopes out of.

ANTIGONUS: True, too true, my lord.
If, one by one, you wedded all the world,
Or from the all that are took something good
To make a perfect woman, she you kill'd
Would be unparallel'd.

LEONTES: I think so. Kill'd!

She I kill'd! I did so; but thou strik'st me
Sorely, to say I did. It is as bitter
Upon thy tongue as in my thought. Now, good now,
Say so but seldom.

CLEOMENES: Not at all, good lady.
You might have spoken a thousand things that would
Have done the time more benefit, and grac'd
Your kindness better.

ANTIGONUS: You are one of those
Would have him wed again.

DION: If you would not so,
You pity not the state, nor the remembrance
Of his most sovereign name; consider little
What dangers, by his Highness' fail of issue,
May drop upon his kingdom and devour
Incertain lookers-on. What were more holy
Than to rejoice the former queen is well?
What holier than, for royalty's repair,
For present comfort, and for future good,
To bless the bed of majesty again
With a sweet fellow to't?

ANTIGONUS: There is none worthy,
Respecting her that's gone. Besides, the gods
Will have fulfill'd their secret purposes;
For has not the divine Apollo said,
Is't not the tenour of his oracle,
That King Leontes shall not have an heir
Till his lost child be found? Which that it shall,
Is all as monstrous to our human reason
As my Antigonus to break his grave
And come again to me; who, on my life,
Did perish with the infant. 'Tis your counsel
My lord should to the heavens be contrary,

Oppose against their wills.
To Leontes Care not for issue;
The crown will find an heir. Great Alexander
Left his to th' worthiest; so his successor
Was like to be the best.

LEONTES: Good Paulina,
Who hast the memory of Hermione,
I know, in honour, O that ever I
Had squar'd me to thy counsel! Then, even now,
I might have look'd upon my queen's full eyes,
Have taken treasure from her lips-

ANTIGONUS: And left them
More rich for what they yielded.

LEONTES: Thou speak'st truth.
No more such wives; therefore, no wife. One worse,
And better us'd, would make her sainted spirit
Again possess her corpse, and on this stage,
Where we offend her now, appear soul-vex'd,
And begin 'Why to me'-

ANTIGONUS: Had she such power,
She had just cause.

LEONTES: She had; and would incense me
To murder her I married.

ANTIGONUS: I should so.
Were I the ghost that walk'd, I'd bid you mark
Her eye, and tell me for what dull part in't
You chose her; then I'd shriek, that even your ears
Should rift to hear me; and the words that follow'd
Should be 'Remember mine.'

LEONTES: Stars, stars,

And all eyes else dead coals! Fear thou no wife;
I'll have no wife, Paulina.

ANTIGONUS: Will you swear
Never to marry but by my free leave?

LEONTES: Never, Paulina; so be blest my spirit!

ANTIGONUS: Then, good my lords, bear witness to his oath.

CLEOMENES: You tempt him over-much.

ANTIGONUS: Unless another,
As like Hermione as is her picture,
Affront his eye.

CLEOMENES: Good madam-

ANTIGONUS: I have done.
Yet, if my lord will marry- if you will, sir,
No remedy but you will- give me the office
To choose you a queen. She shall not be so young
As was your former; but she shall be such
As, walk'd your first queen's ghost, it should take joy
To see her in your arms.

LEONTES: My true Paulina,
We shall not marry till thou bid'st us.

ANTIGONUS: That
Shall be when your first queen's again in breath;
Never till then.
   Enter a Gentleman

GENTLEMAN: One that gives out himself Prince Florizel,
Son of Polixenes, with his princess- she
The fairest I have yet beheld- desires access

To your high presence.

LEONTES: What with him? He comes not
Like to his father's greatness. His approach,
So out of circumstance and sudden, tells us
'Tis not a visitation fram'd, but forc'd
By need and accident. What train?

GENTLEMAN: But few,
And those but mean.

LEONTES: His princess, say you, with him?

GENTLEMAN: Ay; the most peerless piece of earth, I think,
That e'er the sun shone bright on.

ANTIGONUS: O Hermione,
As every present time doth boast itself
Above a better gone, so must thy grave
Give way to what's seen now! Sir, you yourself
Have said and writ so, but your writing now
Is colder than that theme: 'She had not been,
Nor was not to be equall'd.' Thus your verse
Flow'd with her beauty once; 'tis shrewdly ebb'd,
To say you have seen a better.

GENTLEMAN: Pardon, madam.
The one I have almost forgot- your pardon;
The other, when she has obtain'd your eye,
Will have your tongue too. This is a creature,
Would she begin a sect, might quench the zeal
Of all professors else, make proselytes
Of who she but bid follow.

ANTIGONUS: How! not women?

GENTLEMAN: Women will love her that she is a woman

More worth than any man; men, that she is
The rarest of all women.

LEONTES: Go, Cleomenes;
Yourself, assisted with your honour'd friends,
Bring them to our embracement.
   Exeunt
Still, 'tis strange
He thus should steal upon us.

ANTIGONUS: Had our prince,
Jewel of children, seen this hour, he had pair'd
Well with this lord; there was not full a month
Between their births.

LEONTES: Prithee no more; cease. Thou know'st
He dies to me again when talk'd of. Sure,
When I shall see this gentleman, thy speeches
Will bring me to consider that which may
Unfurnish me of reason.
   Re-enter Cleomenes, with Florizel, Perdita, and Attendants
They are come.
Your mother was most true to wedlock, Prince;
For she did print your royal father off,
Conceiving you. Were I but twenty-one,
Your father's image is so hit in you
His very air, that I should call you brother,
As I did him, and speak of something wildly
By us perform'd before. Most dearly welcome!
And your fair princess- goddess! O, alas!
I lost a couple that 'twixt heaven and earth
Might thus have stood begetting wonder as
You, gracious couple, do. And then I lost-
All mine own folly- the society,
Amity too, of your brave father, whom,
Though bearing misery, I desire my life
Once more to look on him.

FLORIZEL: By his command
Have I here touch'd Sicilia, and from him
Give you all greetings that a king, at friend,
Can send his brother; and, but infirmity,
Which waits upon worn times, hath something seiz'd
His wish'd ability, he had himself
The lands and waters 'twixt your throne and his
Measur'd, to look upon you; whom he loves,
He bade me say so, more than all the sceptres
And those that bear them living.

LEONTES: O my brother-
Good gentleman!- the wrongs I have done thee stir
Afresh within me; and these thy offices,
So rarely kind, are as interpreters
Of my behind-hand slackness! Welcome hither,
As is the spring to th' earth. And hath he too
Expos'd this paragon to th' fearful usage,
At least ungentle, of the dreadful Neptune,
To greet a man not worth her pains, much less
Th' adventure of her person?

FLORIZEL: Good, my lord,
She came from Libya.

LEONTES: Where the warlike Smalus,
That noble honour'd lord, is fear'd and lov'd?

FLORIZEL: Most royal sir, from thence; from him whose daughter
His tears proclaim'd his, parting with her; thence,
A prosperous south-wind friendly, we have cross'd,
To execute the charge my father gave me
For visiting your Highness. My best train
I have from your Sicilian shores dismiss'd;
Who for Bohemia bend, to signify
Not only my success in Libya, sir,
But my arrival and my wife's in safety

Here where we are.

LEONTES: The blessed gods
Purge all infection from our air whilst you
Do climate here! You have a holy father,
A graceful gentleman, against whose person,
So sacred as it is, I have done sin,
For which the heavens, taking angry note,
Have left me issueless; and your father's blest,
As he from heaven merits it, with you,
Worthy his goodness. What might I have been,
Might I a son and daughter now have look'd on,
Such goodly things as you!
Enter a Lord

LORD: Most noble sir,
That which I shall report will bear no credit,
Were not the proof so nigh. Please you, great sir,
Bohemia greets you from himself by me;
Desires you to attach his son, who has-
His dignity and duty both cast off-
Fled from his father, from his hopes, and with
A shepherd's daughter.

LEONTES: Where's Bohemia? Speak.

LORD: Here in your city; I now came from him.
I speak amazedly; and it becomes
My marvel and my message. To your court
Whiles he was hast'ning- in the chase, it seems,
Of this fair couple- meets he on the way
The father of this seeming lady and
Her brother, having both their country quitted
With this young prince.

FLORIZEL: Camillo has betray'd me;
Whose honour and whose honesty till now

Endur'd all weathers.

LORD: Lay't so to his charge;
He's with the King your father.

LEONTES: Who? Camillo?

LORD: Camillo, sir; I spake with him; who now
Has these poor men in question. Never saw I
Wretches so quake. They kneel, they kiss the earth;
Forswear themselves as often as they speak.
Bohemia stops his ears, and threatens them
With divers deaths in death.

PERDITA: O my poor father!
The heaven sets spies upon us, will not have
Our contract celebrated.

LEONTES: You are married?

FLORIZEL: We are not, sir, nor are we like to be;
The stars, I see, will kiss the valleys first.
The odds for high and low's alike.

LEONTES: My lord,
Is this the daughter of a king?

FLORIZEL: She is,
When once she is my wife.

LEONTES: That 'once,' I see by your good father's speed,
Will come on very slowly. I am sorry,
Most sorry, you have broken from his liking
Where you were tied in duty; and as sorry
Your choice is not so rich in worth as beauty,
That you might well enjoy her.

FLORIZEL: Dear, look up.
Though Fortune, visible an enemy,
Should chase us with my father, pow'r no jot
Hath she to change our loves. Beseech you, sir,
Remember since you ow'd no more to time
Than I do now. With thought of such affections,
Step forth mine advocate; at your request
My father will grant precious things as trifles.

LEONTES: Would he do so, I'd beg your precious mistress,
Which he counts but a trifle.

ANTIGONUS: Sir, my liege,
Your eye hath too much youth in't. Not a month
Fore your queen died, she was more worth such gazes
Than what you look on now.

LEONTES: I thought of her
Even in these looks I made.
To Florizel But your petition
Is yet unanswer'd. I will to your father.
Your honour not o'erthrown by your desires,
I am friend to them and you. Upon which errand
I now go toward him; therefore, follow me,
And mark what way I make. Come, good my lord. *Exeunt*

ACT V. SCENE II. Sicilia. Before the Palace of Leontes
Enter Autolycus and a Gentleman

AUTOLYCUS: Beseech you, sir, were you present at this relation?

FIRST GENTLEMAN: I was by at the opening of the fardel, heard the old shepherd deliver the manner how he found it; whereupon, after a little amazedness, we were all commanded out of the chamber; only this, methought I heard the shepherd say he found the child.

AUTOLYCUS: I would most gladly know the issue of it.

FIRST GENTLEMAN: I make a broken delivery of the business; but the changes I perceived in the King and Camillo were very notes of admiration. They seem'd almost, with staring on one another, to tear the cases of their eyes; there was speech in their dumbness, language in their very gesture; they look'd as they had heard of a world ransom'd, or one destroyed. A notable passion of wonder appeared in them; but the wisest beholder that knew no more but seeing could not say if th' importance were joy or sorrow- but in the extremity of the one it must needs be.

Enter Another Gentleman

Here comes a gentleman that happily knows more. The news, Rogero?

SECOND GENTLEMAN: Nothing but bonfires. The oracle is fulfill'd: the King's daughter is found. Such a deal of wonder is broken out within this hour that ballad-makers cannot be able to express it.

Enter Another Gentleman

Here comes the Lady Paulina's steward; he can deliver you more. How goes it now, sir? This news, which is call'd true, is so like an old tale that the verity of it is in strong suspicion. Has the King found his heir?

THIRD GENTLEMAN: Most true, if ever truth were pregnant by circumstance. That which you hear you'll swear you see, there is such unity in the proofs. The mantle of Queen Hermione's; her jewel about the neck of it; the letters of Antigonus found with it, which they know to be his character; the majesty of the creature in resemblance of the mother; the affection of nobleness which nature shows above her breeding; and many other evidences- proclaim her with all certainty to be the King's daughter. Did you see the meeting of the two kings?

SECOND GENTLEMAN: No.

THIRD GENTLEMAN: Then you have lost a sight which was to be seen, cannot be spoken of. There might you have beheld one joy crown another, so and in such manner that it seem'd s orrow wept to take leave of them; for their joy waded in tears. There was casting up of eyes, holding up of hands, with countenance of such distraction that they were to be known by garment, not by favour. Our king, being ready to leap out of himself for joy of his found daughter, as if that joy were now become a loss, cries 'O, thy mother, thy mother!' then asks Bohemia forgiveness; then embraces his son-in-law; then again worries he his daughter with clipping her. Now he thanks the old shepherd, which stands by like a weather-bitten conduit of many kings' reigns. I never heard of such another encounter, which lames report to follow it and undoes description to do it.

SECOND GENTLEMAN: What, pray you, became of Antigonus, that carried hence the child?

THIRD GENTLEMAN: Like an old tale still, which will have matter to rehearse, though credit be asleep and not an ear open: he was torn to pieces with a bear. This avouches the shepherd's son, who has not only his innocence, which seems much, to justify him, but a handkerchief and rings of his that Paulina knows.

FIRST GENTLEMAN: What became of his bark and his followers?

THIRD GENTLEMAN: Wreck'd the same instant of their master's death, and in the view of the shepherd; so that all the instruments which aided to expose the child were even then lost when it was found. But, O, the noble combat that 'twixt joy and sorrow was fought in Paulina! She had one eye declin'd for the loss of her husband, another elevated that the oracle was fulfill'd. She lifted the Princess from the earth, and so locks her in embracing as if she would pin her to her heart, that she might no more be in danger of losing.

FIRST GENTLEMAN: The dignity of this act was worth the audience of kings and princes; for by such was it acted.

THIRD GENTLEMAN: One of the prettiest touches of all, and that which angl'd for mine eyes- caught the water, though not the fish- was, when at the relation of the Queen's death, with the manner how she came to't bravely confess'd and lamented by the King, how attentivenes wounded his daughter; till, from one sign of dolour to another, she did with an 'Alas!'- I would fain say- bleed tears; for I am sure my heart wept blood. Who was most marble there changed colour; some swooned, all sorrowed. If all the world could have seen't, the woe had been universal.

FIRST GENTLEMAN: Are they returned to the court?

THIRD GENTLEMAN: No. The Princess hearing of her mother's statue, which is in the keeping of Paulina- a piece many years in doing and now newly perform'd by that rare Italian master, Julio Romano, who, had he himself eternity and could put breath into his work, would beguile nature of her custom, so perfectly he is her ape. He so near to Hermione hath done Hermione that they say one would speak to her and stand in hope of answer- thither with all greediness of affection are they gone, and there they intend to sup.

SECOND GENTLEMAN: I thought she had some great matter there in hand; for she hath privately twice or thrice a day, ever since the death of Hermione, visited that removed house. Shall we thither, and with our company piece the rejoicing?

FIRST GENTLEMAN: Who would be thence that has the benefit of access? Every wink of an eye some new grace will be born. Our absence makes us unthrifty to our knowledge. Let's along.
   Exeunt Gentlemen.

AUTOLYCUS: Now, had I not the dash of my former life in me, would preferment drop on my head. I brought the old man and his son aboard the Prince; told him I heard them talk of a fardel and I know not what; but he at that time over-fond of the shepherd's daughter- so he then took her to be- who began to be much sea-sick, and himself little better, extremity of weather continuing, this mystery remained undiscover'd. But 'tis all one to me; for had I been the finder-out of this secret, it would not have relish'd among my other discredits.
   Enter Shepherd and Clown
Here come those I have done good to against my will, and alreadyappearing in the blossoms of their fortune.

SHEPHERD: Come, boy; I am past moe children, but thy sons anddaughters will be all gentlemen born.

CLOWN: You are well met, sir. You denied to fight with me thisother day, because I was no gentleman born. See you theseclothes? Say you see them not and think me still no gentlemanborn. You were best say these robes are not gentlemen born. Giveme the lie, do; and try whether I am not now a gentleman born.

AUTOLYCUS: I know you are now, sir, a gentleman born.

CLOWN: Ay, and have been so any time these four hours.

SHEPHERD: And so have I, boy.

CLOWN: So you have; but I was a gentleman born before my father; for the King's son took me by the hand and call'd me brother; and then the two kings call'd my father brother; and then the Prince, my brother, and the Princess, my sister, call'd my father father. And so we wept; and there was the first gentleman-like tears that ever we shed.

SHEPHERD: We may live, son, to shed many more.

CLOWN: Ay; or else 'twere hard luck, being in so preposterous estate as we are.

AUTOLYCUS: I humbly beseech you, sir, to pardon me all the faults I have committed to your worship, and to give me your good report to the Prince my master.

SHEPHERD: Prithee, son, do; for we must be gentle, now we are

GENTLEMEN:

CLOWN: Thou wilt amend thy life?

AUTOLYCUS: Ay, an it like your good worship.

CLOWN: Give me thy hand. I will swear to the Prince thou art as honest a true fellow as any is in Bohemia.

SHEPHERD: You may say it, but not swear it.

CLOWN: Not swear it, now I am a gentleman? Let boors and franklins say it: I'll swear it.

SHEPHERD: How if it be false, son?

CLOWN: If it be ne'er so false, a true gentleman may swear it in the behalf of his friend. And I'll swear to the Prince thou art a tall fellow of thy hands and that thou wilt not be drunk; but I know thou art no tall fellow of thy hands and that thou wilt be drunk. But I'll swear it; and I would thou wouldst be a tall fellow of thy hands.

AUTOLYCUS: I will prove so, sir, to my power.

CLOWN: Ay, by any means, prove a tall fellow. If I do not wonder how thou dar'st venture to be drunk not being a tall fellow, trust me not. Hark! the kings and the princes, our kindred, are going to see the Queen's picture. Come, follow us; we'll be thy good masters.
 Exeunt

ACT V. SCENE III. Sicilia. A Chapel in Paulina's House
 Enter Leontes, Polixenes, Florizel, Perdita, Camillo, Paulina, Lords and Attendants

LEONTES: O grave and good Paulina, the great comfort
That I have had of thee!

ANTIGONUS: What, sovereign sir,
I did not well, I meant well. All my services
You have paid home; but that you have vouchsaf'd,
With your crown'd brother and these your contracted
Heirs of your kingdoms, my poor house to visit,
It is a surplus of your grace, which never
My life may last to answer.

LEONTES: O Paulina,

We honour you with trouble; but we came
To see the statue of our queen. Your gallery
Have we pass'd through, not without much content
In many singularities; but we saw not
That which my daughter came to look upon,
The statue of her mother.

ANTIGONUS: As she liv'd peerless,
So her dead likeness, I do well believe,
Excels whatever yet you look'd upon
Or hand of man hath done; therefore I keep it
Lonely, apart. But here it is. Prepare
To see the life as lively mock'd as ever
Still sleep mock'd death. Behold; and say 'tis well.
  Paulina Draws a Curtain, and Discovers Hermione Standing like a Statue
I like your silence; it the more shows off
Your wonder; but yet speak. First, you, my liege.
Comes it not something near?

LEONTES: Her natural posture!
Chide me, dear stone, that I may say indeed
Thou art Hermione; or rather, thou art she
In thy not chiding; for she was as tender
As infancy and grace. But yet, Paulina,
Hermione was not so much wrinkled, nothing
So aged as this seems.

POLIXENES: O, not by much!

ANTIGONUS: So much the more our carver's excellence,
Which lets go by some sixteen years and makes her
As she liv'd now.

LEONTES: As now she might have done,
So much to my good comfort as it is
Now piercing to my soul. O, thus she stood,
Even with such life of majesty- warm life,

As now it coldly stands- when first I woo'd her!
I am asham'd. Does not the stone rebuke me
For being more stone than it? O royal piece,
There's magic in thy majesty, which has
My evils conjur'd to remembrance, and
From thy admiring daughter took the spirits,
Standing like stone with thee!

PERDITA: And give me leave,
And do not say 'tis superstition that
I kneel, and then implore her blessing. Lady,
Dear queen, that ended when I but began,
Give me that hand of yours to kiss.

ANTIGONUS: O, patience!
The statue is but newly fix'd, the colour's
Not dry.

CAMILLO: My lord, your sorrow was too sore laid on,
Which sixteen winters cannot blow away,
So many summers dry. Scarce any joy
Did ever so long live; no sorrow
But kill'd itself much sooner.

POLIXENES: Dear my brother,
Let him that was the cause of this have pow'r
To take off so much grief from you as he
Will piece up in himself.

ANTIGONUS: Indeed, my lord,
If I had thought the sight of my poor image
Would thus have wrought you- for the stone is mine-
I'd not have show'd it.
LEONTES: Do not draw the curtain.

ANTIGONUS: No longer shall you gaze on't, lest your fancy
May think anon it moves.

LEONTES: Let be, let be.
Would I were dead, but that methinks already-
What was he that did make it? See, my lord,
Would you not deem it breath'd, and that those veins
Did verily bear blood?

POLIXENES: Masterly done!
The very life seems warm upon her lip.

LEONTES: The fixture of her eye has motion in't,
As we are mock'd with art.

ANTIGONUS: I'll draw the curtain.
My lord's almost so far transported that
He'll think anon it lives.

LEONTES: O sweet Paulina,
Make me to think so twenty years together!
No settled senses of the world can match
The pleasure of that madness. Let 't alone.

ANTIGONUS: I am sorry, sir, I have thus far stirr'd you; but
I could afflict you farther.

LEONTES: Do, Paulina;
For this affliction has a taste as sweet
As any cordial comfort. Still, methinks,
There is an air comes from her. What fine chisel
Could ever yet cut breath? Let no man mock me,
For I will kiss her.

ANTIGONUS: Good my lord, forbear.
The ruddiness upon her lip is wet;
You'll mar it if you kiss it; stain your own
With oily painting. Shall I draw the curtain?

LEONTES: No, not these twenty years.

PERDITA: So long could I
Stand by, a looker-on.

ANTIGONUS: Either forbear,
Quit presently the chapel, or resolve you
For more amazement. If you can behold it,
I'll make the statue move indeed, descend,
And take you by the hand, but then you'll think-
Which I protest against- I am assisted
By wicked powers.

LEONTES: What you can make her do
I am content to look on; what to speak
I am content to hear; for 'tis as easy
To make her speak as move.

ANTIGONUS: It is requir'd
You do awake your faith. Then all stand still;
Or those that think it is unlawful business
I am about, let them depart.

LEONTES: Proceed.
No foot shall stir.

ANTIGONUS: Music, awake her: strike.
                    Music
'Tis time; descend; be stone no more; approach;
Strike all that look upon with marvel. Come;
I'll fill your grave up. Stir; nay, come away.
Bequeath to death your numbness, for from him
Dear life redeems you. You perceive she stirs.
    Hermione Comes down from the Pedestal
Start not; her actions shall be holy as
You hear my spell is lawful. Do not shun her
Until you see her die again; for then
You kill her double. Nay, present your hand.
When she was young you woo'd her; now in age

Is she become the suitor?

LEONTES: O, she's warm!
If this be magic, let it be an art
Lawful as eating.

POLIXENES: She embraces him.

CAMILLO: She hangs about his neck.
If she pertain to life, let her speak too.

POLIXENES: Ay, and make it manifest where she has liv'd,
Or how stol'n from the dead.

ANTIGONUS: That she is living,
Were it but told you, should be hooted at
Like an old tale; but it appears she lives
Though yet she speak not. Mark a little while.
Please you to interpose, fair madam. Kneel,
And pray your mother's blessing. Turn, good lady;
Our Perdita is found.

HERMIONE: You gods, look down,
And from your sacred vials pour your graces
Upon my daughter's head! Tell me, mine own,
Where hast thou been preserv'd? Where liv'd? How found
Thy father's court? For thou shalt hear that I,
Knowing by Paulina that the oracle
Gave hope thou wast in being, have preserv'd
Myself to see the issue.

ANTIGONUS: There's time enough for that,
Lest they desire upon this push to trouble
Your joys with like relation. Go together,
You precious winners all; your exultation
Partake to every one. I, an old turtle,
Will wing me to some wither'd bough, and there

My mate, that's never to be found again,
Lament till I am lost.

LEONTES: O peace, Paulina!
Thou shouldst a husband take by my consent,
As I by thine a wife. This is a match,
And made between's by vows. Thou hast found mine;
But how, is to be question'd; for I saw her,
As I thought, dead; and have, in vain, said many
A prayer upon her grave. I'll not seek far-
For him, I partly know his mind- to find thee
An honourable husband. Come, Camillo,
And take her by the hand whose worth and honesty
Is richly noted, and here justified
By us, a pair of kings. Let's from this place.
What! look upon my brother. Both your pardons,
That e'er I put between your holy looks
My ill suspicion. This your son-in-law,
And son unto the King, whom heavens directing,
Is troth-plight to your daughter. Good Paulina,
Lead us from hence where we may leisurely
Each one demand and answer to his part
Perform'd in this wide gap of time since first
We were dissever'd. Hastily lead away. Exeunt

END

Lightning Source UK Ltd.
Milton Keynes UK
UKHW040651220820
368549UK00025B/1058